Praise for Diane & Healing Bodies Healing Souls

I just finished reading "Healing Bodies, Healing Souls: Tools for Self-Transformation" by Diane Gysin. This title should be changed to "Enlightenment 101!" In her literary debut, Diane uses a firm, loving, nudge to cover all the bases to teach the art of self-empowerment in an easy step by step format. Even the highly evolved would benefit from this basic refresher course. I certainly did!
– *Linda Crose-Andersen, MMsc, MH, author of Amazing Grace: A spiritual journey from addiction to enlightenment*

My closest friend in the world was going through an incredibly devastating period, really at the end of her rope, and randomly (intuitively) found Diane online.

Diane performed an hour and a half healing chakra cleansing on her, while reading intuitively why Lee was going through what she was going through and what HER part in it was. My friend's recovery was so tangible it was as though someone had performed life-saving surgery on her.

Honestly, it was so unbelievable that I had to go see Diane myself for a session! Diane is an incredible healer and person. I don't care how far you have to drive to see her, it will be the best thing you can do for yourself and those you love. – *Cat M.*

Words cannot express how amazing Diane from *Healing Bodies Healing Souls* is. This place is a true gem in Fremont, and I advise anyone who is interested in self-improvement to give this place a try—it is LIFE CHANGING!

Before discovering meditation class with Diane, meditation was always something I wasn't sure if I was doing *right* or if I was actually doing it at all.

Diane uses a unique technique to guide you along some of the most powerful meditations you will ever experience. And even after just one class, you will leave feeling nothing short of AMAZING!

I HIGHLY recommend Diane's meditation classes and energy work at Healing Bodies Healing Souls. Attending her classes is the best decision you will ever make! – *Michelle S.*

Diane is an amazing human first of all. I will never forget that experience or how deeply she can see what needs to be healed.

I could barely walk up those stairs to her office, and almost cancelled because I just couldn't handle the pain I endure every time I walk ANYWHERE!

When I left, I carried my cane instead of it carrying me. My mind was clear and hopeful that there would be less pain physically and mentally— I was reborn! Thanks again Ms. Diane, you haven't seen the last of me. We will take a journey again. Now I'm writing my story instead of living everyone else's. – *Sherry C.*

Tools for self-transformation

Diane Gysin

Copyright © 2015 by Diane Gysin

ISBN-10: 1511601531
ISBN-13: 978-1511601535

Date Published: July 26, 2015

The author would love to hear from you.
DianeG6870@aol.com

Logo and cover art by Megan Wood (TangledArtOnline.com)
Editing, book design by Len Hodgeman (lenhodgeman.com)

Dedication

To my daughters, Megan and Erin. The universe has gifted me with two wonderful daughters who have shown me what life is really meant to be. I know I would not be who I am today if I had not received these two gifts of a lifetime.

To all my family and friends, who have supported me in this unique life I have created.

To Mike Tracy—you have been the one man, perhaps without knowing it—who has expanded my awareness and believed in me more than I have believed in myself. You mean more to me than you will ever know.

Acknowledgments

I would like to honor my Mom and Dad, and the life that they have enabled me to have. They taught me to work hard, a gift that has made me who I am, and one of the things I love about myself.

To all my friends and clients that have laughed at my uniqueness and added value to my world! I love your support that you have given so freely.

To my spirit teachers for helping me evolve.

Jenelle C., for the times you gifted me by just listening.

Michelle S., who has been a gift to me in every sense since you walked into my office.

Melissa I., for helping proof my book.

Luke B., for the coaching class that re-inspired me.

Billy G., for offering your support and friendship.

Jeff S., for being my one male friend that has stayed with me for years.

Contents

Introduction	1
Write one success story	7
The healing power of meditation	19
The power of the aura	33
Learning about your Chakras	47
Working with a Life Coach	69
My body, my temple, my strength	83
The Law of Attraction	95
Manifesting personal goals	111
Hypnotherapy	121
Case studies	131
Bring it all together	151
About the author	164

Introduction

I have been teaching and healing for over 25 years, studying many different modalities in order to improve my understanding of time, space and energy. I find learning is a never-ending joy.

As a life coach, healer, hypnotherapist and intuitive reader, I love researching ways to bring more joy into our lives. My goal is for you to read this book and learn to incorporate these powerful ideas into your own world.

I want you to become aware of life and the energy in and around you, learn to be aware of the moment—the here and now—that represents present-time and space, because that's really all we have. Learning to shift into a higher vibrational energy can help create miracles in your life

This book will help you understand the importance of being self. It's time to learn to be real and in the moment. It's time to understand that all the labels that you have been given in the past have held you back. We are all evolving on a daily basis. You no longer need to see yourself in terms of those old labels. You are as high as you can dream. So get ready and learn to dream higher.

I am giving you permission to be who you are, and to like what you find. This work that I challenge you to do is worth it. Stop seeing yourself through the eyes of others. You are the only one in charge of your happiness and your outcomes. Together, let's rewrite our stories, find strength and focus on becoming better and better.

Now get ready for a beautiful shift of perception and energy. Just breathe, enjoy yourself, dream high and read on.

I personally celebrate my gifts often and focus on redesigning myself. I feel it's important to challenge my belief system to continue to grow. My two daughters, my life and my career are what make me want to become more enriched and balanced.

This book can help you to become more self-aware. You will learn tools that will assist you in understanding and creating a healthier life path.

After each chapter you will have two questions designed to create a space of change. One question will help you create a thought that will serve your higher self. The other question will help you create an action that can start a new path.

I'd like to introduce you to a few terms that we will be using in the following chapters.

Vibration is an energy that is constantly moving and changing with our mood, our thoughts and the foods we eat. All emotions will shift our vibration. The vibration is how we feel our energy. All living things are made of energy. The higher your vibration can be, the healthier your physical body will be.

Aura is the energy coming from within the body, radiating throughout the body and around the physical body. This energy field changes and shifts with your emotions. For overall wellbeing, it's important to learn to clean and protect your aura from outside influences.

7 Major Chakras are your energy centers, each with a different vibration, sound, and color. Each chakra has a layer of energy within the aura. So, to be energetically healthy you need to have your aura and chakras in relative balance. This will create your space of being more energetically healthy.

The Law of Attraction is another way of understanding energy and its vibration. Our thoughts become emotions that are projected into our world creating our outcomes. What we think about, we attract into our lives. The Law of Attraction emphasizes thinking about the positive things we want to bring into our story.

Reiki is a form of hands-on healing. Through attunements, one person's body is able to transmit energy to another body for healing purposes. The body wants to heal and balance itself so Reiki gives the body extra energy to heal at a faster rate.

Hypnotherapy works with your subconscious mind to create a healthier story. People have negative stories that they bring into the present-time. Writing a positive story and having it sink deep into your subconscious, that has present-time goals, can help you expand your life very quickly.

Prana is life force energy that keeps us alive and breathing. Prana can be harnessed from the wind, the earth, the sun and the water. It's an energy that is extremely powerful, and in that powerfulness, very healing.

Havingness is when you look at your life and realize that you want to require more of yourself in life. To raise your level of energy, to embrace and to have more in life.

Poverty Consciousness is when you run fear-based energy on money and abundance. This is a low vibration and thought pattern that keeps people from manifesting higher dreams.

Knowingness is when you have deep belief in an area of thoughts. When you know something without a question attached.

Spiritual Transpersonal Release Technique
Once known as Retro Clearing and endearingly referred to as a spiritual Roto Rooter, this is one of the most powerful therapies on the planet. It transfers powerful consciousness and energy to the recipient allowing them to heal. People feel, and will notice, a fast and quick energy release of negative patterns

This includes past lives and any unseen negative influences as well. Many of our fears and phobias often do not have any base of origin in this life. Our mental and emotional bodies are affected by unseen spiritual forces in positive and negative ways. It is time to open to the positive and heal the negative.

Write one success story
Believe in yourself and create one outcome.

As a teenager I experienced two life-threatening moments: a farming accident and a car accident. Either one could have resulted in my death.

I consider myself blessed that I had the focus and drive to create successful outcomes in both situations.

The summer I was 17, I was driving swathers and tractors for my parents' family business. (A swather is a large machine for cutting hay.)

This particular day, I was cleaning out the front end of a John Deere swather when it was suddenly turned on. I guess no one noticed I was on my knees, waist deep inside the front end, cleaning out the dirt that clogs the blades.

As the front end took hold and the huge, extremely powerful blades began to turn, I held on to the bars as tight as I could to try to prevent them from cutting me. They could easily have sliced my guts right open.

The belts and gears on the sides of the swather were jumping. I knew I was not strong enough to physically freeze up the swather but somehow I did. Finally someone turned the engine off. I was pulled out by my dad completely unharmed! It took me a few minutes to laugh it off, and then I crawled back in and got back to work.

During that moment of time, once I understood what was happening, I did not panic. I was able to stay 100% in present-time. In that split-second, I created that one successful story and outcome I wanted. This moment of being fully present saved my life. Because I was able to hold onto that one story, I was blessed enough to live and survive to tell my story.

Staying focused on one success story, holding pure intent in the moment, focusing on the outcome I wanted, saved my life.

As the swather tried to pull me into the header, I told myself, *If it's my time I will crawl out and die instantly.* I was okay with dying if it was my time. I knew that I really couldn't cheat death.

I also told myself, with full knowingness, *I will not die this way. I will not die having my guts ripped out in front of my parents.* I kept repeating it, *I will not die this way, if it's my time, I will crawl out and die.*

I could not do that to my parents. I was okay with dying, but not that way. On an energetic level I identified with spirit, not with my physical body.

I took full control over my outcome and it was a beautiful feeling. I was actually spirit, and in spirit form there is no time and space.

I did not focus on my past history or my future in that history, I was just in that moment. Pure present-time gave me the power to stay focused and to own my outcome. Years later I can still remember the feeling of being focused and dialed in to present-time. I have drawn power from that moment continuously, and have had many more amazingly powerful moments that have given me the ability to focus and be strong. I know you can create the same kind of moments for yourself.

Was it a miracle? Yes, and it was not going to be my last one!

You also have the power to learn how to create magical moments. It's all within us. You can find your strength and write the outcome you want and never entertain a second outcome. You can do this in a split-second.

Notice that I did not write two or three additional stories. Any story other than the first one would not have been the success I wanted. This would have weakened my outcome and questioned my desire for success. I just kept repeating to myself, *I will not die this way*. That thought gave me the power to control my outcome.

Never falter in these moments. Never question your sense of power. It's a weakness you can't afford to have. Trust me, you have more power than you can ever imagine. Now is a good time to create a knowingness that you have power in your words, and power in your body that works with your intent. This will help you to create a strong spiritual practice.

A word of caution: When you create higher goals and dreams, be careful who you share your visions with. I tend not to tell a lot of people what I'm working on. I don't want their judgments to cloud my thoughts. I do not want peoples' narrow mindedness to change what my truth is. I'm very selective in who I confide in. I only open up to people that have a positive mind, and that can hold space for my dreams. This concept alone will help you stay on your own true path. *You deserve it!*

When you have doubts or fear, you lose control of the result you desire. I did not entertain the idea that I was 17 and that this was impossible to do. It would have lowered my vibration and changed my outcome.

* * *

I was challenged again just a year later. I was involved in a bad car accident. I was taken to the emergency room and told I was fine. I would probably have a headache and should just take some aspirin. No tests had been done and I was sent home.

But when I woke up the next morning, my left eye was completely closed and swollen over the bridge of my nose. It was bashed in. My forehead and the top of my head were enlarged. My right eye was half closed and was extremely light sensitive.

I couldn't even brush my hair because of how sensitive my scalp was. Over the next three days I became black and blue all over my forehead, left cheek, and my chin, as well as down the back of my neck and shoulder.

My instincts told me I needed to move very slowly. I was not sure what was going on, but I would know the details later on.

The next day I was to fly to Mexico to meet my parents for a family vacation. I was so disfigured in my mom didn't even recognize me. I kept telling myself, *This is not a problem, this is not an issue*. My parents never go on a vacation and I refused to ruin this one. I dismissed everyone's worries and did not let them change my story. Again I was able to write the story I wanted to live out.

My family was very worried. People that saw me in Mexico cringed when they noticed me. I knew I needed to stay focused on the outcome I wanted. When everyone asked how I was doing, I mostly ignored their concerns. I was going to be fine and this was not an issue.

Telling myself and my body that this was not an issue, showed my body that it could handle the healing I needed.

That was my way of creating the ending I wanted. I never in any moment of time allowed myself to entertain another outcome. Why allow another result to come into my thoughts and pull me away from a fully successful story?

When I got home I went to my chiropractor. It had been two weeks since the accident and my neck was stiff, my eye was still black and blue and was very bloodshot. My chiropractor was shocked that no medical procedure had been done the night of my accident. He asked if he could take an X-ray. After seeing the X-ray he then sent me to a neurologist.

I survived a completely cracked open skull, a massive concussion, a hemorrhaged left eye and a blood clot over the left side of my forehead and brain. The neurologist could not believe that I lived without having any medical care. They could not believe I was in a pressurized airplane with a cracked skull, blood clot and concussion without having serious medical issues occur.

Had my neurologist seen me that night, I would have had surgery. They would have put two plates in my head to pull the skull together, reconstructed the forehead and drained the blood clot. I can't imagine the trauma my body would have had to endure. With my success story, I'm blessed. The doctors said, "No surgery needed!" *Yippee, I did it again.* I was able to successfully live to tell an amazing healing story.

They sent me home to continue to heal on my own. My body was in full healing mode. I'm very thankful the original doctors sent me home. I understand most people would have and should have had surgery. Many people have not learned to heal themselves, I understand this—but I can. And of course, I have no long lasting issues from my accident.

The mind and body can be very powerful. Every body wants to heal itself and stay in balance. Your body can heal itself with time and positive energy. With the power of the mind and healthy energy, the body will heal itself and find balance. Your energy and thoughts behind your words can create the space needed to overcome moments of life-threatening events. I've been blessed to live this. If you have any form of medical emergency, please do what you need to do to become healthy.

It feels good for me to have a sense of strong presence in my life. This has come into play many times. It does not have to be a life threatening moment to call on your powers. This gift can be used in many ways.

* * *

Here's another success story via a client: a massage therapist came in for an energy session. She needed to improve her business and create more income. My goal was to focus on getting her energy in line with her real desires. The first thing I needed to do was to center myself and be neutral.

I was cleaning her aura and chakras when I asked her how many clients she would like to have per week. I wanted to energetically set her up for success, create abundance and set her vibration for her goal. She responded with the number 10 and as a professional massage therapist myself, I thought 10 was very high. I have been certified for 12 years but I average three to five per month. I never looked at that part of my business.

When I showed her my reaction to the number of clients, her response was, "It's only two per day." In that moment I was running clean energy and was not invested in my past or my future information. So I was able to look at her information and manifest the same into my own world. I wanted that!

As I looked at her petite built and little arms, I thought to myself, *If she can do it, I can do it, I want to do it, I'm going to do it*. Again, I was not part of my past or my future. I was not looking at this through my limited stories. I was able to completely manifest 10 plus massages per week, within five days. It took me three seconds to set my intention and energy and five days to really see it manifest. Success can be that easy and that fast.

People tend to focus on negative thoughts. Now you know the importance of being positive. Don't get trapped in negative thought forms, low vibration and a negative lifestyle and than wonder why the results are less than desirable. You now know that writing one success story and releasing all negative thoughts will create a sense of personal power. That personal power is the tool for your new successful life. It's time to refocus your intent by creating more positive energy in your world.

All three stories have the same theme for me. I chose one outcome and did not falter from my desire. I never for a moment thought I could not achieve my stories. The cleaner your energy is, the stronger you are emotionally and energetically, the easier it is to achieve your outcome.

It's important to learn to run your own energy and not go into agreement with other people's stories about your life. You have your own answers when you listen to yourself.

When you cannot hear your own answers, you have been overly influenced by other people's energy dominating your own space. Meditation and energy work will help you understand how to become a stronger, happier you.

When you choose to be self-empowered, you will find that there is NO person that can stop your greatness—Not even yourself. This is when you are connected to a higher source and a higher self.

What thoughts came up for you that will help you embrace a *One Success Story* outcome from this moment on?

What stories can you change that will serve your higher self and create the life you want?

The healing power of meditation
What is meditation and why is it important?

Meditation can be a life-altering practice. A regular practice will help you become a stronger more powerful person. When you create a space of balance you will notice less stress, a healthier mind, and an increased state of self-awareness. You will also be able to open your heart and cultivate compassion. This will help you become a better story writer for yourself. As you meditate, your mind becomes clearer and you will find yourself more in charge of the quality of life that you create.

Meditation will help you start to tune into your own thoughts and hear your own questions answered. I want you to understand, you're more powerful than you have imagined. This will help you become empowered and happy. Your power will help you along your own personal path. This is a perfect way to go within and find your true self.

Learning to sit quietly and deprogram yourself from your past is vital. You are no longer that sad school child, the lonely kid or angry adult.

So, who are you now? Meditation will help you find yourself again. Now it's time to gain your personal power. Relaxing and enjoying life is essential to living fully. Here are a few ways to become centered and balanced. All you really need is a few minutes of your time.

Meditation is a way of releasing the static in your mind; the clutter, or noise that stops you from hearing your own intuition. Relaxing and focusing on yourself will allow the healing answers to come into your subconscious mind. You will be able to hear your answers. It's an amazing gift to give yourself.

Practice and it will get easier over time. Your mind needs to release years of built-up clutter. This may take time, so keep moving forward. Your body can re-learn how to relax and release the old programming that you went into agreement with years ago. Just allow yourself time to come back into this present moment. Your happiness level will start to increase, and a sense of peace will develop. It really is a win-win situation.

Meditating is a way of being still and without thoughts. It's a process to get there and you are worth the time. You have no need to rush this process. Just enjoy where you are and where you want to go. No judgement. This is a practice that is enjoyable. Please do not worry about rushing to make meditation happen. It will just happen.

Okay, I hope you can start to open into the idea that you have more control of the outcome of your stories. You create your reality and you are the only one that is in charge of your happiness. If you are not fulfilled in life, look in the mirror and see where you are and where you want to be. You need to want to work through your story so you can live a fuller life. Being happy is your birthright. Claim it!

The universe has enough abundance to go around. It's time for you to be more invested in life. I want you to desire more out of life and create more greatness for yourself. *What does that mean to you?* Meditation will help you clear your thoughts focus on your truth and find your higher path.

We, as a society, need more happy and successful people to help empower this world. Helping yourself also helps everyone around you. I'm excited for you to learn tools that will spring board you into higher consciousness.

You will be less stressed, less rushed and more centered. The only thing one needs to start is a place to relax. This chapter will give you tools to incorporate meditation into your everyday world. I also recommend finding a meditation group. It feels good to be around like-minded people and the energy can be amazing to witness.

* * *

It's time to start shifting, cleaning out your old energy and becoming more empowered in the here and now. You will notice this helps quiet the mind and body. It's a perfect way for you to understand what kind of thought forms you gravitate to. Are you more positive or negative? With meditation you can learn to let go and release negative thoughts and energy that keep you stuck in your problems.

Your practice will bring you a sense of peace; a feeling like life is working for you. Just 10 minutes a day can help you refresh your body, mind and soul. I think you can find 10 minutes a day. You have to get out of your normal routine to create any kind of new outcome.

Stop and ask yourself, *Am I ready to create new positive ways that will benefit all areas of my life?* I know you bought this book because you want change. Now take these simple steps and change your life.

A cleaner mind and a more balanced body will have a better energy field. Once you start to meditate on a regular basis, you will see huge results. Meditate on your own or find a group. Just start today and take control over your life.

I have witnessed many moments when people find that quiet place during meditation. It's a beautiful moment to witness. I see faces soften, bodies relax deeply, and a sense of peace that melts into their world. They may have walked in feeling relaxed but they had no idea how the body hides stress and emotions.

So many people have had great improvements in their life. When you feel more relaxed you handle everyday pressures better. Stressful moments no longer take over your whole world and it becomes easier to let go. You will also find you no longer feel the need to suffer with stress.

Maybe you want a healthier peaceful mind, less stressful body and lifestyle. Focus not on where you are, but where you want to be. Don't worry about how you will achieve your outcome. The universe is listening to your vibration. During meditation, let the universe know what you desire in life.

Learn to incorporate meditation into more of your day-to-day world. Meditation does not always have to consist of sitting down quietly. You can, and will, learn to do meditation in everyday activties. These occasions of empowerment will manifest into more areas of your life. I want you to see more beautiful moments in your normal world. I want your positive energy to be your new main focus.

Some notice after mediating that they are more productive and calmer in body and mind. Many people see relationships become amazingly healthier. When you can let go of stress energy, your life improves. Your health can improve greatly. It's easy to get trapped into a thought that is less than desirable. Let's change that with a soft heart. Change is good.

When I meditate often, I am much more balanced within my own emotions. This is when you are present and focused on a successful life. It's time for us to learn to be in charge of our emotions and not be subject to a lower vibrational energy. Meditation is an easy modality to learn. I know you will enjoy the outcome.

* * *

A meditation client asked one evening if she could share her success story. Holly is married with two small children and needed to learn to relax. She said she was coloring with her five year old daughter when she said, "Mommy, thank you for not yelling at me so much anymore." Meditation allowed Holly to relax and let go of her stress.

Previously she had allowed her kids to frustrate her and then let her frustration out on her kids. She also learned to be more present in her life by not dwelling on the past or worrying about the future. She learned to enjoy herself more. Her husband personally thanked me for helping her because he noticed that her meditation has also helped them in their marriage.

* * *

"I didn't know I was so screwed up," was one client's response after a month of coming to class. She was able to release bad habits and a tendency to toxic relationships. This put her more at peace, enabling her to focus on herself and her own desires. She is now focused on her success and is writing books and selling them worldwide. Meditation classes helped her ignite and see her passion.

* * *

Another client was meditating to set and reach her one-year goals. She said that within a one-year period, she had accomplished all her goals. During a meditation class she envisioned herself a year into the future. She could see herself looking amazing, feeling happier than ever, and successful in her business ventures.

During that year she took control of her health and fitness. She went on more adventures in her free time. She grew her new business. Even her hair looked the way it did in her vision. Exactly a year later, she realized that she was now living proof of her vision from the previous year. Without this class, she might not have even set goals to achieve. You can use meditation as a way to be positive and goal focused.

So, let's start.

I will give you a few ways to become centered and balanced. All you really need is a few minutes of your time.

Find a comfortable space, breathe deeply and softly, close your eyes while allowing your body to become deeply relaxed. Feel the tension in your physical body. Now just allow your body to soften more, to relax more and to be less guarded in the moment. While you are relaxing take notice of your mind and see if you can just let go of thoughts that are outside of this moment. Can you just relax? Can you let go of your worries? Have your worries taken over your whole existence? Interesting, huh?

I recommend just laughing at yourself. It's healthier to laugh then to get frustrated. Again, frustration is negative, so stay upbeat and positive. That's the direction we want to go. Remember, life should be fun!

Spend a few minutes continuing to breathe, deeper and slower while you relax any tension you may have in your body. Enjoy the power of the breath. Now feel yourself in the room, feel your surroundings. Be present and allow time to slow down.

This is a good state to be in. Enjoy this moment as long as it feels good to you.

While sitting in silence, release any thoughts that may come through. Remind yourself of your body's age and be okay with the number. It's your reality. This will help you become aware of time.

Now with your eyes still softly closed, see your surroundings by picturing them in your mind. This will help you with space. Understanding time and space will help your body learn what present-time really is.

It's the here-and-now feeling. When body, mind, and spirit are connected with time and space, we can start creating a very powerful transformation.

* * *

You should always create a grounding cord that will connect you to the earth's energy. A grounding cord is a link that you imagine starting from the base of your root/first chakra and continuing all the way from your body to the center of the earth. Run all your energy you want to release down the grounding cord. This will keep your room energetically clean and other people around you clean.

Envision a grounding cord: It could be something like an oak tree, a beautiful rose quartz crystal, a large rope or anything that is easy for you to imagine. Let's play with an oak tree grounding cord for now.

Become aware of your first chakra, red in color, also known as the root chakra, close to your tailbone. This oak tree is connecting in and around your first chakra. Picture the base of the oak tree going through the floor into the earth. Now picture the roots growing deep into the ground. You now have a strong connection to Mother Earth.

You are now ready to release any and all energy that no longer serves your highest self. Envision the energy you want to release as going down your grounding cord. Release energy from your day or week; from work, or relationship issues that do not make sense to hold onto and store in the body. You can also release all energy that you have outgrown and all energy that is not yours. Continue to release for as long as you feel the need. Each time you meditate it's important to keep releasing energy down your grounding cord.

Enjoy being relaxed and present in your body. This is a perfect time to become aware of your goals and desires. Being relaxed and feeling good helps you to write powerful dreams. Remember to see yourself as happy and positive with your life. Feel your body become healthier in this moment.

Enjoy the outcome that you want in this present-time moment. Feel the success. See and feel what it will be like to have your outcome manifested in the here and now. Enjoy the overall feeling of completion. Witness the pleasure in the moment. During this manifestation you want to awaken your body to feel its completion.

Now, go back to that soft feeling, back to being relaxed. Focus on your relaxed body breathing softly. Set your intent to create a beautiful, healthy and emotional happy life with abundance. Breathe, enjoy this moment for as long as you wish.

After a deep meditation I recommend drinking water to ground your physical body. Focus on being kind to yourself for the next few days while your body and energy is shifting into a higher vibration. And always follow with loving-kindness towards yourself.

Meditation in everyday Movement

Meditation in movement is when you become so focused on a single action that all thoughts go away. The body and mind become one in the moment.

Runners after a while get so focused on the run, all else falls away. Create a lifestyle that helps you enjoy life fully.

Rock climbing, karate, dancing, singing are all actions that require one to be focused in the present-time. This is a great way to empty your mind from all the clutter. Find something that you are passionate about. This will raise your vibration and help your energy become stronger and brighter.

How can you incorporate meditation into your life?

What actions do you need to change or add that will give you time and space to meditate on a regular basis?

The power of the aura
I need nothing, I am complete.

Your aura and chakras are two separate energy systems that work together. The aura is an energy field around the body that radiates from deep within the body going outward. It shifts with your mood and health.

The chakra energy centers are confined within our bodies, and will tell the story of your life. They are discussed in the next chapter.

The aura is a magnetic field of energy that is constantly changing and shifting. It reflects your well-being and your emotional health. The aura also reacts to the physical and emotional environment around you. Your aura will shrink, weaken and become diminished when you are feeling unsafe or intimidated. It will also enlarge, shine and become stronger when you feel confident.

People that have a strong presence have a powerful and healthy aura. You have the ability to change your own energy field to create more balance.

All humans, animals, and plants have auras that radiate energy. All emotional, physical, and mental health can be detected from the aura. The healthier the vibration, the healthier your body is. Learning to stay clean and protected is vital for overall health.

A human aura is made up of seven major colors that represent the seven major chakras. Each chakra has a different color, sound and vibration. Each of the seven layers in the aura represents one of the major chakras. These all need to be in harmony to create balance.

You do not have to see the aura to be able to read or sense its vibration. When you notice someone, you automatically have a knowingness based on the energy they are projecting. Without consciously trying, you pick up on the energy they are running.

Your energy reacts whether you are aware of it or not. Learning to be more attuned to others' energy will help you to understand the automatic energy shifts in your own body that happen in response to their energy. You will come to know why your mood changes, and how to not be so reactive.

The more like-minded energy two people have, the stronger your connection is. That is why a shopaholic bonds with another shopaholic almost instantly. Or a single parent with kids will feel a connection with another person with the same story. You both have vibrations that feel similar and comfortable to the other person. Similar energy does not always mean healthy energy.

So many different emotions throughout your day will shift your energy. Learning to have a stronger aura will help you find a sense of balance. It's wise to not have your aura respond to all outside influences throughout your day. The aura has volumes of information about a person's mental, emotional, and physical wellbeing. If it's constantly changing, your mood can swing and create an imbalance. Imbalance creates an unhealthy mind and body.

When your aura changes throughout your day because of others, you will, in effect, become energetically "dirty." Learning ways to avoid matching other people's energy will help you remain more balanced. A balanced body will have a cleaner aura.

Your aura can have low, depleted, congested or dirty energy. Some energy can quickly change back to balance within moments. Some will need to be cleansed and shifted back into a healthy balance. The time needed to create balance again can depend on how long you have been stuck in a low vibration and how long you went into agreement with the story that caused the low vibration.

To keep your aura healthy and vibrating, stay focused on your thoughts, mood, environment, and emotions.

Waking up each day and seeing the positive in your life will help shift your aura into a healthier space. Remember your aura reflects your present-time mood. It can shift quickly with clean, powerful intentions. Checking your moods and emotions throughout your day will keep your energy flowing well and can help manifest a healthier day.

Looking at the positive things around you, focusing on your goals and being kind to yourself will help the health of your aura. Identify and light up in your mind the positive things around you. Goals will help you create a positive place to dwell.

* * *

Salt baths will help cleanse your aura and balance your mental and physical body. A bath is beneficial because water is very healing. Rock salt helps even more because it will absorb the energy being released into the water, keeping your bath water clean. I recommend one or two baths per week, for at least 20 minutes. This is an easy way to start creating a healthier energy body. If you do not have a bathtub, you can rub the salt on your body while showering.

Fresh air and being in nature are natural ways of becoming energetically healthy. Our outside elements can be healing. The sun-prana energy, wind-prana energy, water-prana energy and earth-prana energy on your body are natural ways of balancing your energy and becoming grounded to our earth.

When you begin to understand that you have power over your energy field and health, you empower yourself. Being empowered creates a new awareness, the awareness that you can now start to change your outcome. You have the power within you to have greatness.

People carry emotions that are transmitted for all to pick up. It's like a radio wave that is being heard on a subconscious level. That frequency has a vibration that shifts your energy field. Learning to protect yourself will keep you strong.

One way to avoid this is by bringing in your aura closer to your physical body to stay cleaner. When your aura radiates too far from your physical body, you will be more susceptible to others' moods and health information.

When you become aware of your energy or when you are alone, have your aura extending about three feet from the body.

When I'm around people or in my office, I want to have my aura close, one to two feet from my body to keep myself balanced. This helps me create a safe way of keeping my energy clean.

When I can keep peoples energy outside of my own energy field, I do not pick up on whatever emotions they may be running. I can stay more balanced within my own space.

Take a moment, and with your inner voice, ask your aura to radiate out from your physical body three feet. Witness the feeling of your aura close. Now, ask your aura to come in two feet and witness how that feels. It's that easy and that quick. Don't second guess the shift. Just accept that energy can move that easily and quickly.

I feel emotionally safer when I am able to keep others out of my aura. If you notice that you start to feel nervous with others around you, call in your aura and do not stand close to others. Just imagine your aura as a bubble coming in tighter around you.

When you're in a place of business, standing in line close to strangers and you feel uncomfortable or feel like your mood is changing, pull your energy in close.

When you listen to someone's story your energy can shift. It's important to learn to simply listen, and to not be brought into the emotion that they are experiencing. If they are angry, sad or frustrated, don't take that information into your aura. It's their story and experience, and you do not have to match its vibration.

Don't allow yourself to open up your past emotions while listening to someone's story. If you hear a negative story, don't go into your bank of memories, recall the emotion and bring it into your present-time vibration. It's not wise to match their energy in that moment. That does not benefit anyone. Learn to stay neutral and just witness their story. In witnessing, you can stay in the present moment and be strong for all involved.

It's important to allow people to have their human experiences without you trying to fix them. When you try to fix them you become emotionally invested in their outcome. This is when drama is created. It's not your outcome or story to be involved in. Becoming invested in another person's experience is not necessary and will create a dirty energy environment for you. Good or bad, it's best to stay detached from other people's personal outcomes.

Learning tools to avoid becoming subjected to other's emotions will help you maintain your own vibration energy and not take on their vibration. Witnessing them tell their story, without becoming involved in their experience or invested in the outcome, helps you create a healthy emotional boundary.

Some people are not ready to shift and change. Trying to fix them is your demise, not theirs. Let them learn and go through what they need to experience for a life lesson. They might not be ready to change and the more we are okay with that, the healthier we will all be.

It is important to your overall health to learn to work with your energy field so that you are able to witness but not match other energies. We no longer need to get so invested in others that we lose ourselves.

Now that you are not going to match other people's energy, you can focus on yourself. Now the real fun begins. I want you to be empowered to move forward in your own life.

Write goals and start empowering yourself. Create high dreams and goals that will raise your own energy field into a higher vibration. Higher vibrational people have more positive energy. Winners win because they automatically run that belief system of success. They have learned to take care of themselves.

Some people tend to dwell on past moments. They go back into a negative time and keep reliving this moment again and again and again. It feeds their negative energy. If your past has fear, anxiety or negative-based energy, your aura will stay depleted.

Break the cycle and release the old stories that hold you back. Cancel out the negative stories that plague your thoughts. Learn to embrace thoughts that will bring you into a better space. It's difficult to create abundance when you deplete your own energy.

I want you to cancel out any dwelling on these stories and learn to stay in present-time. *Your past is over, leave it alone!* Dwelling will only deplete your aura. A depleted aura is a low vibration. A low vibrational aura keeps you stuck. It's a no-win situation.

* * *

Colors have a strong presence in the energy field and will shift with the colors you choose to wear for the day. Look at the colors you have around yourself and see what you can do to brighten up your outside world and create a brighter inside world. It's hard to have a bad day when you surround yourself with bright colors. When drawn to a particular chakra color, you are working with that one energy center. It's best to incorporate all seven colors into your life for balance.

Surrounding yourself with positive, loving people and being in a positive environment is crucial to a healthy aura. The more you can rise into a higher vibration, the higher the gifts are. It's all about feeling worthy of good energy and good people.

When you run negative or positive energy in your energy field, it needs to be fed. Negative energy needs negative hits all day long. Positive energy needs positive hits all day long. Whatever you run is what your focus is on.

A negative person needs to focus on all the negative things around them. The negativity needs to be continuously fed. The traffic is bad, the weather is too hot or too cold, and the Starbucks line is moving slow. Everyone is in a bad mood and nothing can be done right. If you run negative energy you light up all the negative things and moments around you that will help feed your negative state. That's what you are wired to view and become.

Positive energy needs to be fed by positive energy. You become attracted to the good things around you. Your overall awareness of your surroundings feels good and you see the good around you. Traffic may be slow but you don't notice it. The weather might be too hot or too cold but you're not affected by it. Life feels good and you see all the good around you. Your smile attracts other smiles. It's contagious in a positive way. This is where our focus creates a positive outcome.

This is a great space for creating your greatness. The more you feed yourself and others with positive energy the more positive energy flows through you. Now you can create abundance, health, and happiness. This is when your aura is healthy and full of life force energy.

Be a positive person and see everything as positive. Check in with yourself and see who you are. Become aware of your aura shifting into balance. This is when you become aligned with your higher energy and your higher self. This is when life is good.

It's important to check in with yourself often and notice whether you have chosen to run positive or negative energy. This awareness will help you shift when you need to shift or help you to stay in your greatness.

Learning to focus on the positive will give you the outcome you desire.

The world needs more positive and enlightened people.

What can you do to create healthy boundaries with friends and family?

What actions can you commit to that will help you stay outside of others' stories and stay focused on your own outcome?

Learning about your Chakras
I go within and I come out with answers.

The word chakra literally means energy wheel. Your chakras are your psychic centers, located inside your etheric energy body. They are not something that one sees with the physical eye, but something that is 'viewed' psychically, or intuitively.

When you start to work energetically on the chakras your life will quickly begin to shift. Meditating and visualizing the chakras will help create the change you desire.

Your body has seven major chakras and thousands of minor chakras running throughout your etheric body—the energy field surrounding you that stores information about your physical body.

The major chakras run along the center of the body, from the base of the spine to the top of the head.

They are like spinning vortices that create the energy that influences our lives.

The chakra's energy is created by a whirling motion inside each individual chakra center, which is a vortex energy center that may spin clockwise or counterclockwise. The shape and size of the chakras change depending on your emotional energy body. The more positive the energy is, the larger and stronger the chakra becomes.

Most of our life experiences can be viewed within the energy of the major chakras. They continue to store information that governs our outcomes.

The minor chakras have more to do with our physical bodies. They have stored energy that contains information for a specific part of the body. For example, if the knee chakra has a low vibration, the physical knee will have a physical issue.

Our life's emotional and physical energy history can be adjusted by healing the chakra's energy. Through meditation and energy work, we can go into agreement to no longer hold onto past information. This will help bring your energy into more present-time health.

Letting go of old information, that no longer serves your higher self, will create the healing space needed. Releasing past energy enables you to move away from stories that you have outgrown.

When you start to work with your chakras it's best to work with all of them. I did a phone reading and noticed my client's chakras were all small except for the fourth heart chakra. When I mentioned this to her, she was surprised because she always worked on her heart chakra, not the other chakras. However she always worked to open her heart chakra to bring in more love. That created the imbalance.

If you only give one chakra all your attention the other six will become diminished. It's like having seven children and giving only one child all the love and attention.

Chakras work best when they are all balanced and working within the same amount of energy. Each and every chakra has a purpose that can help you grow into balance.

* * *

The colors of the seven major chakras correspond to the full light spectrum. These colors have a profound effect on our physical, mental, emotional and spiritual energy body. The different shades of color will signify the different degrees of health. Brighter energy means healthier and cleaner energy.

When a chakra is balanced and healthy, it is a vibrant shade. When all of your chakras are balanced, they are roughly the same size.

The seven chakras also create a yin-yang energy, where the upper chakras are more for cosmic energy and the lower chakras have to do with earth energy. It's very important to have both equally balanced.

The heart chakra, 4th chakra, is the bridge that brings both upper and lower chakras together. This is your heart center or chakra center.

When you work with the upper chakras, you run more cosmic energy. That creates a spiritual connection. If you run too much upper chakra energy, you will be very connected to higher energy but not enough in the here and now.

When you work with the lower energy chakras you run more earth energy. If you run too much lower energy you will be so grounded that it can be difficult to create change in your life. It's important to learn to balance all your upper and lower chakras in order to be energetically balanced.

For example, an accountant might run low chakra energy, and tend not to have a lot of upper chakra creative energy to call on. Whereas an artist or healer might run high chakra energy, but tend to have difficulty remaining grounded, balanced and stable.

In either case, in the extreme, it can be like a body builder only working the upper body or lower body and allowing half to be stagnant or underdeveloped, causing an imbalance in the body's muscular system.

Learning to maintain, heal and balance your chakras will help create better outcomes for your future. Healing the energy in your chakras will open you up to new energy growth resulting in new present-time opportunities.

This shift will allow you to move away from living old stories that result in the same stuck patterns in your life, creating the same old outcomes. This is where you can benefit from energy healings.

When you go into deep meditation or prayer, it will raise your consciousness. You will become clean and thoughts will become clear. The chakra energy can then flow upward, bringing with it a higher state of awareness. When chakras are not blocked or impeded, energy will run freely from the base of our spine to the top of your head, through each major chakra center, creating a oneness within our energy system.

Let's start at the first chakra, and begin to learn and understand how to work with each of the seven chakras that create our energy system.

1 - Your Root chakra

The root chakra, or base chakra, is located at the perineum, or base of the spine, and is represented as having four petals. Its color is red. This chakra is the base platform that you create from, and the source of your survival, prosperity and abundance.

A healthy first chakra creates a solid foundation for your being, and allows you to feel safe and protected in this lifetime.

This is the chakra that connects you into Mother Earth's energy, providing a feeling of being in the here and now, a place for creating the prosperity and balance that you desire and the place where abundance dwells. When you are grounded to earth energy you will feel and experience a feeling of being safe, which will help you to move forward into fulfilling your innermost desires.

You will want to focus on creating a larger platform through your first chakra. A small, unhealthy chakra would be like having a small box to move inside of. A healthy chakra is a nearly infinite stage to move upon and create from. Embrace the idea that the universe has room for each person to have what they need, and that you can ask for your own greatness. You have been born for greatness.

The root chakra is deeply connected to a person's prosperity. People that 'run' (focus on) poverty consciousness are unable to run the healthy amounts of energy needed to create the outcomes that they want. If they make good money they tend to lose it or waste it, creating negative energy that immediately takes the prosperity away.

You cannot have poverty consciousness and prosperity at the same time. Be wise, and learn to shift your first chakra energy into its natural healthy state.

Create your own knowingness that you have the power to shift your life into a place where your deepest desires may begin to unfold.

Meditate on creating a healthy desire that will manifest in the here and now.

Embrace the idea that you can ask and receive more greatness and abundance.

This is the time and place to write your dreams and goals in a larger, fuller spectrum way than you ever have before.

See yourself bringing in abundance. Feel yourself grounded and being in present-time and space with earth energy. The here and now is where we create our safety. Relax and be open to receiving.

And so it is ...

2 – Your Sacral Chakra

The sacral (or navel) chakra is located in the abdominal area, between the base of your spine and your navel, and is represented as having six petals. Its color is orange.

This is your sex chakra, passion source, male/female God/Goddess energy, and creative energy. This chakra is important for maintaining a healthy balance in your personal development.

A balanced second chakra will create a positive body and mind for a creative and healthy relationship with yourself and others.

Coming from a balanced chakra will give you a healthy outlook on creating, or birthing new ideas, owning your own sexuality and your God/Goddess energy. This center gives you the space to be an individual by helping you to see yourself as a strong spirit.

An unhealthy second chakra will create inner conflicts and sexual problems, lowering your overall energy into a simple need for power. But a healthy second chakra involves owning who you are and provides the drive you need in order to be passionate about your life, your creative endeavors and your relationships.

We are born to be sexual creatures and society has not supported the full spectrum of this natural state of being. Each person needs to find their own power in being a strong sexual male or a strong sexual female in this lifetime. It's your divine right.

We need stronger people in this world running their power (creative) energy. It's not about force or overpowering others, but it is about owning and knowing your own personal power and how to use it. A healthy sacral chakra will give you a backbone in life, a sense of presence and a sense of being in the moment. Embrace being a powerful spirit.

Meditate on creating self-empowerment in your actions.

Be who you really are; a confident, vibrant spirit.

Now picture yourself becoming more and more alive and free.

Raise your vibration and springboard yourself into being truly filled with passion, creative energy, and power.

3 – Your Solar Plexus Chakra

The Solar Plexus Chakra is located a few inches above the navel in the solar plexus area, and is represented as having ten petals. Its color is yellow.

This chakra is the source of your self-love, self-acceptance and self-confidence. It's where healthy boundaries and self-honoring are nurtured.

A healthy third chakra creates a sense of personal empowerment, gives you high self-esteem and a strong awareness of self.

This is where we care for our own personal needs. A healthy third chakra will allow you to move from always having to be in control to the freedom of not needing to be the one in control of all situations. You can find the critical balance of being centered and present that will guide you into being confident in your own personal belief system and unique path, when your solar plexus chakra is healthy.

A dirty third chakra will create low self-esteem and constant personal struggles. When you stop living your purpose this chakra becomes depleted. You start to question yourself and become stuck in negative stories. You give away your power, resulting in a powerless life.

Meditate on loving and being non-judgmental to yourself.

Learn to release the idea of the ego, and become more of your own support person.

Start cultivating self-love and self-acceptance from within.

Work on relaxing into your authentic self and being OK with who you are in this present-time.

You will find your life becoming more emotionally balanced when you work on your third chakra. People will notice your greatness more because you love yourself more. This will improve your whole sense of wellbeing.

4- Your Heart Chakra

The heart chakra is located in the chest cavity or heart area and is represented as a lotus flower with 12 petals. Its color is green, and green is the color of love.

The heart chakra is the center chakra that bridges the upper and lower chakras together.

The heart chakra's divine qualities are love, compassion, kindness, forgiveness, and purity. This is the place that transcends pure love.

This chakra creates a space of unconditional love for others. Our heart center balances our loving kindness, so we can see the world in a loving way.

Imagine someone coming up to you with a cute little puppy or kitten. Your heart chakra opens up and responds with loving kindness. This shifts you into a space of witnessing love and gives you a warm heartfelt feeling.

When the heart chakra gets dirty or congested with other peoples negative energy, or even your own old stories, you tend to experience the world as unloving and uncaring. You will feel life is negative and constantly find yourself in no-win situations.

It's important to understand that life is good and it's always moving forward, to feel blessed and to have so much to be grateful for. When you can run being grateful you can align yourself with higher powers.

When you start to work with the heart chakra, you work from a heart connection, a true space of love.

Meditate on loving kindness. See it spreading throughout time and space.

Send love to yourself and all the people that have come into your life's path.

Remember to send loving kindness to the ones that tend to change your heart connection.

Just experiencing more green in your world will help to open the heart chakra.

When we meditate with the heart chakra we want to clean out any energy that has past pain attached to it. We no longer want to see life through dirty glasses. We want to see life with clean and healthy present-time information—Yes, through rose-colored glasses.

It's incredibly liberating to open your heart chakra and expose yourself to more greatness. More greatness will allow your true self to heal and will also help the world to create balance.

5 – Your Throat Chakra

The Throat Chakra is located in the throat and thyroid area. This chakra is represented as a lotus flower with sixteen petals. Its color is blue.

This is your communication center, where you energetically speak and hear words. It's the place where your energy becomes attached to your words.

Remember everything is energy. Your words have an energy vibration that is transmitted when you speak or listen to words that have been spoken.

Your ability to hear and speak with clear intent starts in this chakra. Being conscious of how words have energy attached to them will help you become a stronger communicator.

When working with a healthy fifth chakra you will be able to listen and speak wisely from your own higher truth. It's best to not assume that you know what others think. We hear and understand accurately and completely from our own space, not from another's space or viewpoint.

Communication is vital to our sense of wellbeing. We energetically communicate on so many levels. We hear things wrong when the energy is not clear or coming from present-time. Being in the present moment will help your communication come from more of a grounded space.

A healthy Throat chakra will create a strong powerful voice that wants to be heard. When you feel more confident in speaking, you know you are grounded in present-time truth. This is the space to connect with people in a healthy way.

We know it's important to connect to people and the way we connect is mostly with words. Being confident in our style of communication takes a strong and confident person. It's wise to breathe and always speak your truth, and own who you are and what your personal belief system is.

When you have a problem connecting with a person, they might not own enough of their fifth chakra to be able to speak their own truth. It's not like they are consciously lying, but it's simply their need to keep someone else comfortable by denying and being unable to see truth.

Meditate on your fifth chakra to open yourself to communicating from your present-time body's wisdom.

Find a place that is your present-time truth and breathe into that information. This will give you the confidence to speak clearly in the here and now.

Find your own truth that needs to be heard.

6 – Your Third Eye Chakra

The Third Eye Chakra is located at the center of your forehead at eye level or slightly above. This chakra is represented as a lotus flower with two white petals. Its color is violet to indigo, and it is your connection to your 'mind's eye,' to higher knowingness, intuition and psychic powers.

Working with your third eye will help you connect with your own higher consciousness and hear your own answers to your questions.

Learning to clear your sixth chakra from outside influences creates a space for you to hear your own words. This is a way of self enlightenment and of connecting with your own innate knowledge. It's the way to go inside and hear your own voice.

When you want to focus on your own answers and have clarity in moving forward you will want to use your sixth chakra. This energy center has the ability to give insight and clarity to your desires. The more you can clear this chakra from other influences, the more you can hear what your divine truth is.

In meditation focus on clearing out other people's energy from your sixth chakra. In other words, clean out the voice, the power, and the control people try to have over you. You no longer need to entertain that they have power over your thoughts.

You do not want to automatically accept others' information and energy as truth for you. Once you can own your own space, you will create a healthier and more balanced outcome based on your own truth and not on outside influences.

This is a very powerful space for you to be in. Your own answers that serve you will always be the best for all involved. It's no longer important to make everyone happy and sacrifice yourself.

It's important to know, when you make a personal decision that you only need to worry about your true self. A personal decision is for yourself and your own outcome.

We no longer feel that we have to keep others happy in order to keep ourselves content for the time being. We now make ourselves happy and allow others to respond accordingly. This will be amazingly freeing for you.

People tend to want to tell you what is best for you. For example. I recently mentioned to a friend that I wanted to buy a truck. He automatically started to tell me why I didn't need a truck and why I shouldn't buy one. I'm thankful I knew he did not have my truth to guide him and that I should not entertain *his* idea of what *my* own truth was.

It's important to stop letting people take charge of your outcome. Your own inner voice will have your true answer and you now want to follow your own energy.

Meditate on owning your energy—That will align you with the information you're seeking.

This is a place of personal power and it's time to empower yourself.

7- Your Crown Chakra

The seventh chakra is located at the top of the head and is represented as a lotus flower with one thousand petals. Its color is violet to white and refers to enlightenment. This is the space that transcends pure consciousness, a feeling of being awakened and having infinite intelligence. This is a start to a life path of spirituality.

The seventh chakra helps connect you with your divine, or God energy. This is the place of devotion and spiritual awakening. It is your connection to the Gods, Goddess, higher energy, spirits or whatever divine energy you believe in. This chakra connects you into the universal or cosmic energy.

A healthy seventh chakra will give you a deeper connection with your spiritual self. Maintaining a healthy seventh chakra gives you a spirit connection to a higher source of information and creates a feeling that you are not alone. Your high vibrational connection of energy can flow through you to open you up to receiving high information.

During meditation or prayer you will connect with energy from the universe to balance and heal the body, hear your higher information and be able to channel spirit.

Clearing your crown chakra will enable you to connect with the divine power that can guide you. When you ask to be guided, you open yourself to receiving information that will give you clarity in life. Once you ask, it's important to silence the mind. This will help the information come into your consciousness.

When the mind is silent through meditation or prayer, you become open to receiving the answers you need to help you move forward in life.

Your higher spirit guides will assist you on your path.

Allowing yourself to be guided opens you up to the cosmic energy that has all of your answers.

Advancing your Chakra work with stones.

Each chakra regulates a layer of your consciousness. If a chakra is blocked it needs to be stimulated. Here is a list of stones that can help the energy be restored naturally. The color and energy of each stone will resonate to each chakra, helping to restore balance and harmony in mind, body and spirit. These stones can be used in meditation to empower your meditation practice by placing the stone close to the associated chakra.

Chakra	Chakra Stone
Crown Chakra	Ametrine, Sugilite, Lilac Lepidolite, Amethyst or Clear Quartz
Third Eye Chakra	Amethyst, Tanzanite, Charoite, or Sodalite
Throat Chakra	Lapis Lazuli, Blue Lace Agate, Larimar or Turquoise
Heart Chakra	Rose Quartz, Green Aventurine, Morganite, Kunzite or Emeralds
Solar Plexus Chakra	Citrine Crystals, Golden Labradorite, Amber, Honey Calcite or Golden Yellow Apatite
Sacral Chakra	Orange Calcite, Orange Carnelian, Vesuvianite, Crocoite, Amber or Golden Topaz
Root Chakra	Red Jasper, Red Aventurine, Red Garnet, Red Calcite, Ruby or Black Tourmaline

What changes could you have if you focused on each energy chakra?

What changes can you shift to find time for yourself and the life you want?

Working with a Life Coach

Stay invested in yourself. Become an empowered you!

A life coach is a professional who is dedicated to guiding you into a healthier, more fulfilled life. Someone that can help you understand what you need in order to grow, change, and continue on your life path.

The problem is that we all create habits and then get stuck in a story that does not serve our present-time needs and desires. That's why it's so important to redesign ourselves on a regular basis. This means looking at our life and seeing what needs to change and what we want to stay the same.

Working with a life coach can provide a new perspective on who you are, where you are in your life and where you would like to be. It's like creating a bridge from where you are to where you want to be.

Your coach can assist you in creating and manifesting your new, more positive stories. Old stuck stories are one reason you are not achieving your life goals. Let's release those thoughts and focus on you, as you exist in the here and now.

It's extremely empowering to release old stories, ideas, and dreams that have not grown with you. Letting go of them will give you more energy for creating the new you.

So many people become trapped in the same low vibrational story and create the same old low vibrational outcome. As a life coach, I want to encourage you to write better dreams for a better future.

You are no longer tied to your past stories. You are now becoming a new and healthy present-time success story. *This is your divine right.*

As a life coach, I listen to people's stories and help them become aware of the vibration and the theme that connects everything together. I will question the truth of your stories by asking you whether it's really necessary to keep that thought pattern. Find out if your story is really your truth. This can be very powerful.

Once a thought is questioned and looked at in present-time, change can often be so simple yet so powerful.

Through this process, you will become more aware of how your story sounds in present-time. You may reevaluate what you thought was a good story, and find the power to change the story, and thus to change the outcome.

Friends will usually adjust to your old themed stories, simply accepting them as your truth. To them, it's just you being you. Generally, they don't know how to question you and push you to the place where you really see the full consequences of the entrapment your story has resulted in.

They listen to you, but are not able to push you out of your automatic storytelling and into a different mindset. This is what is required to mix up and challenge your *stuck in the past* automatic responses.

* * *

You no longer have to be your past story. You are not your past, you are always what you choose to be. The stronger you are with yourself, the stronger and easier you are able to shift into a new you.

We will create new stories, which will become your new truth. This change is actually quite easy once you start getting excited about the possibility of a new outcome.

We all live our stories out, whether they're good or bad. Now is the time to own your power and create the outcome that is necessary to expand your future.

* * *

Now look at the areas of your life that you want to change.

Let's write your first new success story. I want you to know how good it feels to gain control over your thoughts and actions and to take healthy feelings and catapult them into action.

Don't concern yourself with too much of your past stories. You've told your negative stories so many times that you actually believe that they are still real. It's time you just stop. I will not witness a story that holds you back. Remember that your past is gone, and embracing the here and now feels delicious.

Now envision you're in front of me ready to change your outcome. Pick one area that you're tired of recreating the same unwanted results. Now see yourself telling me what you want. Please remember, tell me what you want only, not what you don't want. I understand this part can be confusing because you have not previously written a new positive outcome. Stay focused on your desires.

Stories that you have written in the past may not have had a lot of positive energy attached to them. This is the perfect moment to witness a change in your story writing. Focus your mind, your thoughts, and your energy on the desires that you want to fulfill.

Write this with passion, with a new sense of greatness and with a new knowingness. See yourself being able to receive this at one hundred percent. Write from your heart chakra with loving kindness attached and from your third chakra for self-love and self-acceptance.

Some people tell me they just want to be happy. But, what does happy mean? It's too broad a concept to have any real meaning. What area of your life requires more happiness? You may need to re-evaluate your desires and find the specific areas in your life that require more happiness.

Do you feel passionate about something? Tell me where your passion becomes ignited. Coaching can help bridge the gap from where you are to where you want to be. If I can get you out of your automatic excuse story, then together we can find way out of this "I'm stuck" manner of thinking.

Here are a few common themes that tend to hold people back:

- I can't leave this bad relationship.
- No one is hiring now.
- I'm too old.
- I'm not good enough.
- It's hard to raise kids as a single parent.
- Life's tougher for me than for others.
- I'm never going to be successful.
- I have no support.

Know that you have a divine right to be happy. Often people are just not focused on a positive outcome. Happy people, own the right to be happy. They own power and they have a lot of bragging rights.

You *can* leave a bad relationship, get a well-paying job, feel good about yourself, and raise great kids regardless of how bad your current circumstances may appear. This is your healthy truth. The only thing that stops you from creating a successful outcome is your need to own your negative story. Now write a new, successful one.

Dreamers dream of beautiful outcomes. Dwellers dwell on past mistakes. I want you to want to be a dreamer in moving forward in your life. Let no one stop you from living your purpose.

A successful person makes a quick decision and an unsuccessful person doesn't feel good about owning a decision. Be the successful one!

Start by creating in your mind one healthy success story. One positive story can help ignite your passion and draw you into the next positive success story. This will start building momentum. Remember, it's your success story that you want to create and build on—Not a story that people give you. Most people will never dream high enough for you.

I often tell my clients to flip a coin. On the other side of your negative story is the success you desire. So now, think of an *excuse* you have been hiding behind.

Flip a coin and see the other side of your story. Write a new healthy outcome and know you are now becoming that person. Believe in yourself. Learn to sell yourself your own greatness. It may sound too easy but in all honesty, it really can be that simple. Start with one positive success story and build more from there.

Flipping a coin to see the other side of the situation and starting a meditation practice are two of the tools that will help you rewrite your outcomes.

You are the star of this story. You always have been, you just hadn't yet given yourself the starring role.

Now you can change your outcome. Start to demand more out of life. Focus on becoming more and more healthy in body, mind and spirit.

Repeating stories that no longer serve you here and now is just a waste of time and energy. This needs to stop. Don't go back into your old routines that hold you in the past. Your past is gone. So now, how bad do you want to change? I know it's connected to your *havingness* level and this is why it is important to the universe that we are all equal in deserving greatness.

I like to think of my past as though I'm in an airplane trying to look back at my life. An airplane cannot go in reverse, so too, I cannot go backwards and relive any past moments. There is no path to find. I cannot even revisit it or try to retrace my path. So I just look out onto my horizon, my future, and my change. This is a perfect way to stay focused on where you want to go and how good you want it to be when you get there.

Good things can and do happen often. Look around you. We have a lot of successful people in the world. They run the energy that creates a positive mind and spirit. Why? Because they believe that greatness happens, and in that moment they are not experiencing fear-based thoughts.

A healthy person does not wake up every morning and question whether or not they will live a healthy life. They have a knowingness that it is just that. They run healthy energy. The more you can create the belief that greatness is achievable, the faster you can become your more powerful self.

I remember years ago, meeting a young lady on her eighteenth birthday. In her mind she had big plans! Her success story was to quit school as a high school senior and work full time at her present-time job. She was so excited, and believed she was doing something great.

Her goal was to quit school to work full time at Donut King. My heart broke. I wanted her to have higher life goals. I wanted her to see more possibilities for herself. I wanted someone in her life to show her that she could have more. I wanted someone to show her what a successful life looks like. She wrote a story that did not have a lot of future success attached to it.

I ran into her a couple months later and she was now disappointed that she had quit school. Her dream had not fulfilled her expectations. Now think of your goals, and *double* them and then *triple* them.

Go for the gold! Be bold enough to ask for more greatness in your life!

Start questioning areas of your life where you feel stuck. Being stuck is a low vibration energy that does not help you in moving forward. Start to feel good knowing that you are creating a new outcome. Get excited and know that once you start to feel positive, it's easier to move forward.

I want you to know you are not trapped into staying in a relationship, a job, or marriage. It's your own belief system that holds you back. We are never really stuck in the purely physical world. It's the mental world that traps us.

We are conditioned to stay stuck even when we are not happy. There are no physical chains that keep you in that situation. It's your belief system that is holding you hostage. You *can* move, and now *will* move into a healthier place. *Believe in yourself and in life.*

You know, we tend to become lost in our personal world. Then we get complacent in that lost feeling.

Then we get trapped within the feeling of that commonness. Until we learn to rewrite our story, we will always keep becoming smaller and smaller in our story in order to make do with the expected small outcome.

Breaking down the invisible ties that hold you prisoner and becoming who you were born to be. This is the power of you being you. Creating that success story will direct your energy into becoming better and better.

This is now your goal. This is the key to your happiness and self-empowerment. Now we can see the authentic self coming into greatness, and you have the freedom to create.

Look around you and see other successful people. See how success looks on them. Match the energy vibration and style they run in making themselves successful. They run high vibrational goals for themselves and write only one success story again and again. That one first success story gave them the outcome and foundation to build another one on.

Get excited to witness people that have achieved their goals. They run the energy that manifests the outcome you desire for yourself. It's in the power of their mind and the energy that they believe in. It's a beautiful energy to witness in others.

I have an amazing friend who is highly driven for success. He doesn't need to think *about* success. He doesn't *worry* about success. He simply *owns* success energy in his mind, energy field, body and actions, and in his everyday world.

When I'm around him for even a brief moment, I start to run, and to feel, more success energy at a higher level than ever before. He inspires me to push myself out of my own comfort zone and to ask for more. I completely admire his driving force of success.

It's important to surround yourself with like-minded people. People that can inspire you and make you want to be a better person. Become more invested in the thoughts that are always creating your reality. Take charge in your own world. It will feel better than being complacent.

Our lives are a reflection of how much time and value we give ourselves. You are worth all your energy and more. Your life is worth fighting for and you now can achieve more than you have ever thought possible. Starting here and now, know that you have the divine right to ask for more.

When you have finally come to a point in time where the old patterns of life are no longer comfortable, then you're ready to change.

Let this moment be the moment that changes your life.

Find your power and move into your space of greatness.

It's time to fill the world with more positive and like-minded people. Let these words empower you, your family, and your future.

What area are you ready to challenge and re-write?

What actions can you commit to that will help you become more in charge of your story?

My body, my temple, my strength
I now understand where I want to go and that's within.

Your mind has to create a healthy story that will create a healthy outcome. Understand that your energy is your power source to pull from. This is where you create the agreement for change.

Your body is the place where your spirit resides. This body/temple will be your dwelling as long as your spirit is evolving on earth. In order to keep yourself powerful in body, mind and spirit, you need to honor this temple.

Learning to handle stress, keeping the body moving and having a healthy lifestyle will help the body. This is a sacred place that when it's fed can be the most cherished gift you can give yourself.

Life comes from having a physical body. Without your body, you are no longer here on earth, living life. Let's learn to go within and honor what we have been gifted with and create a better experience while we are here. This is important to understand for our whole spiritual, physical and life connection.

Taking special care of our human body's gift is honoring who we are spiritually. The more we honor our bodies the healthier our spirit can be. We need our bodies to exist, and they should not be ignored or taken for granted.

Most people know how to take better care of themselves and just don't. Now is the time to start understanding how important our body is to our existence.

Life is meant to be lived in balance. Finding quietness and peaceful moments will nurture your life. We are not meant to be inside, breathing recycled air or lighting up our life with unnatural lighting. Understand in these times it can be hard to be in nature but I want it to be a goal. I want you to be outside more and understand that being outside will nurture your body and mind. If you want a healthier body you will find ways to give it what it needs. Being outside is a perfect way to find balance from a soul level.

Moderation might be the best rule to apply. We live in an environment that is not always *health-focused.* We do not need to live in a healthier place to be healthy. You have more power over your life no matter what is happening around you. Taking charge needs to become an obligation for you to obtain a healthy body, mind and spirit. We can no longer allow ourselves to use others or our environment as an excuse for ignoring our temple. Becoming self-empowered will give you the strength you need to find your personal power.

In nature, energy is all around us and available to feed our own life source energy. Nature offers us a clean source of power to draw from. We have wind-prana energy, sun-prana energy, water-prana energy and earth prana energy to balance out all areas of our lives. This prana energy feeds the body and heals our emotional, mental and physical levels.

When you meditate, ask the body what it needs that you have not given it yet. We have a third eye that we see from and a third ear to hear from. Soften your thoughts and let your third eye guide you to what your body needs so you can listen and receive a higher source of information. The third ear will help you hear the answers you need to move forward.

Tuning into your third ear's information can be a powerful source of knowledge. When you tune in to your sense of hearing, your own voice speaks to you. You have so much information on what your truth is that comes from deep within you. Learning to tune into this sense of inner hearing can be a guiding force in your moving into your own sense of power.

Know that any information that you can receive needs to be acted upon. This will strengthen your mind to listen to your third ear's information, to hear when your higher self is speaking to you. You are one with your body and mind when you can connect to the inner ear.

I receive a lot of information from my third ear. The third ear can help me hear my own higher self talk, and can guide me into a higher place. This is where I want to be.

In that moment, I know my own answers. It's my one truth that comes from deep within. The cleaner I am, the less resistance I have and the less ego my mind has to silence. I'm able to hear my third ear's information more clearly. Learning to relax, breathe and listen helps me become more open to being guided.

It really is that easy once you find your focus.

The energy around us can affect our physical body by lowering the vibration of our temple. Keeping the aura close will help protect the body from reacting to its environment. When you are in a dirty environment remember to bring your aura in close—as close as you need to in order to ensure that no one is standing within your space. I have at times had to bring my aura in as close as three to four inches.

We know stress can kill the body. It's been proven that stress ages the body and tears down the immune system. It's important to your quality of life that you focus on the overall health of your body. Your goal is to learn to handle the stress with little or no long term damage.

We can no longer just accept stress and stay there. Life moments will happen and we can still stay in a healthy energy field. We need to learn to manage and release the stress that's in our lives. Our bodies need to learn to release this stress for survival.

A stressful moment is just that. A stressful *moment*. A moment is an isolated incident in time. Once that moment is over we need come back into a place of balance. This is when you have power over your outcome.

If the stress is more of a long term issue, we need to learn the coping skills necessary for creating moments that are stress free. Stress can no longer consume your life. In order to stay strong and be successful during these life moments, we need to stay on track with our higher goals. Learning to not stay trapped in a fear-based, stressful moment is crucial to staying healthy. Remember that your life is not defined by one moment of time, it's defined by many moments that add up to create a base story.

Stay focused on your whole life story and not the one area that is being lit up at the moment. This is the time for you to remember to keep the positives and goals that you desire in focus. This will keep your future desires charged. Whatever is lit up and charged the most is being fed and kept alive. Feed your higher vibrational thoughts more than the lower ones. This will bring you into your power source.

Stress may not always be your fault, but your action in not taking care of yourself during this moment is. It's time that you learn to take action, to *not* become a victim during a rough moment, but instead to become stronger then you may have ever thought you could be. Many times life will throw you a curve ball that may seem unfair. But in all fairness, it's actually a moment to grow. Looking at it as a test will help you shift into a more positive position and to overcome this obstacle. It's about seeing the winner in you and writing one success story. These moments become available to you when you are ready to become a stronger person.

When we have painful moments, we have a body and an energy reaction. The aura becomes smaller, the body becomes weaker and the mind goes into survival mode. I want you to learn to look through the stress and see a winner in yourself. You have the ability to turn a stress moment into a success moment. The universe will guide you towards what you feel you deserve. Find that winner energy in you and stay focused on that one success story that you have the right to create.

I recently had an issue with the IRS that dropped me to my knees. I could not stay stuck and in pain while continuing into greatness. *I was not going to be a victim*. I had to fight for myself and my life. After processing my issue, getting the help I needed, I told myself I would come out of this as a winner and be stronger and more empowered than ever before.

I wrote that one success story, keeping my focus on my outcome. I had the desire to win and because of that, I came out as a winner. I gave myself only one option and that was to win. I'm also stronger and more powerful than I have ever been.

Was it fair that I had to go through that? Fair is not part of the equation. Was it a life challenge that I was able to handle head on, win and come out even better and stronger that I thought possible? Yes, and even with all the pain attached, a blessing occurred; and that made me grow.

Creating a healthier you that can create a stronger life can be a natural progression for our spirit to evolve into. It's a mindset and an energy force that we learn to align with.

Stress can also be trigged by poor nutrition. We understand that our bodies need rest and healthy food to operate at their best. Do you honor your body? We know what to do, but do we act on it? Well, it's time to understand the importance of a healthy mind, body and spirit. Nurture your body as if it was the most important gift you have ever received. When you focus on your body's needs, you will want to honor yourself more.

Our bodies are made to move, and they operate best with healthy food. Look at the world you have created and see if you honor your body. It's about balancing life and health.

Your body, your temple, is the vehicle that will drive you to your destination. Without your body you have no connection with time, space and the here and now. The healthier the body, the more we can ask of it.

We want to advance spiritually, but it's tough when we don't have a healthy body to push forward with. I find it fascinating when people come in and complain about the health of their physical body. They get frustrated with the limitations that result from the current state of their body and don't understand why they have limited energy to draw from. Well, they don't take care of the body that houses their spirit.

Medicine, alcohol, prescription drugs, recreational drugs, junk food, stress and life itself can cause the body to shut down. I'm asking you to look at your lifestyle and see where you have the power to overcome the obstacles that hold you back. It's your choice to have, or not have, these obstacles in your life. Don't use them as an excuse for your lack of desire to move forward in your health.

There comes a time when we can no longer look at our crutches and justify them, even to ourselves. This is the opportunity to move into a healthier and more organic lifestyle that will feed our greatness.

It's about owning who you want to be and choosing to be that empowered person. You desperately desire to move forward into greatness, and this is your moment to choose greatness.

It's that easy once we let go of our limitations and accept our greatness. Build trust within your heart, your inner voice, your third eye and your third ear to be the one and only guide.

What can you do to become healthy on all levels?

What actions will you incorporate into your new self that will help you become more empowered?

The Law of Attraction

Be careful what you wish for, the universe hears everything.

The Law of Attraction is very simple. The universe hears and understands all your thoughts. When you worry, the universe gives you things to worry about. When you are on top of your life feeling blessed, the universe gives you blessings. It starts and ends with your story.

Being able to challenge these stories will help define why you are attracting each outcome. Your inside voice has so much power over your outside world.

Your thoughts, your vibrations, and the stories that run your energy can be heard by the universe. The universe is not emotionally invested with the tone of your story. While you entertain your thoughts, the universe is manifesting, at the same time, whatever vibration is connected to your story. Listen carefully to your inner stories, because the universe will manifest them regardless of whether they're positive or negative.

The Law of Attraction is always turned on energetically. All thoughts and vibrations manifest into your own reality. When family members run the same vibration, they match each other's stories; which is why the same issues keep getting created. I'd like you to see your life and career as your own story. If high blood pressure or poor health runs in your family, you do not have to accept it as your own truth. Step back and see yourself without this family story, then build on what you desire your story to be. The Law of Attraction can break your family's ties to a negative story.

Ask yourself: *What family agreements do I have, and do they, or do they not, serve my higher self?* If not, please rewrite your story with the outcome you want. Live by that new statement and watch how your body, mind and spirit can shift.

When someone around you is sick, don't go into agreement that you will most likely get the same cold. If you do, the Law of Attraction will help you manifest the cold. When you are not careful, you match the vibration that is needed to get sick.

Our past programming, which we have matched from childhood or later life moments, has created our belief that we deserve what we get, i.e. we get what we feel we deserve. Then the universe designs our life around that belief. It's time to see what you can create as an individual person with no prior history. This will drastically change your normal outcome. It's time to dream high and believe in the Law of Attraction.

If you felt in your childhood that you were not as smart as your sisters or brothers, your thoughts wrote that information into today's present-time information. As a child you took that information as your truth. That past story now has no real information for your present-time life. You have not, as yet, changed your story into one for your adulthood— and now it is time.

You are no longer that child and now no one can deny you your greatness. Rewriting these stories will help you own the energy of who you are. This will be a way to a better you.

When you change your inner voice, the universe will change your outer world. Start seeing yourself without limits. Start fresh and love being you. It's important to listen to your inner dialog and make your stories more positive from the inside out.

Many people have negative beliefs that they take as truth. For example, most people have been told that if you do not go to the dentist regularly you will get cavities. If this is something that you take as your truth then I would recommend going to the dentist often. However, if you can be a powerful individual and write your own stories, you can create your own truth. I never did believe that I needed to go to the dentist every six months. As an adult, I knew I could take care of my teeth and I did not want to, or need to, match a story with a negative belief. So I went every six years with little or no dental care, and I have very healthy and strong teeth, as I should.

Others have a fear of being successful. They want success, but they have a hard time believing in themselves. The universe is so in tune with your thoughts that you will receive precisely the roadblocks that keep your stories consistent. Your truth may be the one thing that stops you from creating your dreams. Learn to question what you thought was your truth and see what needs to be changed.

When you can release energy that you no longer want to match, everything can change. I meet a lot of couples. Statistics say that about 50% of marriages will end in divorce. If you have that energy in your mind while dating, then you will have the option of divorce in your life and marriage. If you entertain this, the universe can't do anything but align you with a person that will not be your long term partner.

If you want to get married and stay married, then only entertain that outcome. It's about writing one success story and allowing the Law of Attraction to align you with the connection or partner you need.

The Law of Attraction is your winning ticket to positive energy.

We believe in what we tell ourselves and the Law of Attraction is listening. It's now time to commit to a healthier story.

When you were a child, your parents' words had more meaning than they do as an adult. Let's clean up your childhood issues so you can move on. As an adult who is thinking and creating in present-time, we can remove the negative stories that we owned.

Who are you now?

We are powerful spirits that are here to be amazing. We are not low vibrational spirits that struggle. That is not our authentic self.

Focusing on what the Law of Attraction needs from you will help turn your outcome around. Any stories that you entertain need to be surrounded with positive energy. Look at where you are and where you want to be. See the new steps that are needed and build on that success.

Worrying stops your ability to manifest the positive outcome you desire. It is a waste of time and energy. So stop worrying, and focus on the positive result you want.

Keep your focus on your outcome and your eyes on the prize. Each step will get you closer to your dreams. And then you can start another dream. Every time you match the success vibration you will find it easier to be successful again.

In order to change your outcome, we need to change the story you tell yourself and the story the universe works from. If you want better health, project yourself into a positive healthy body. If you want better relationships, see yourself sending love and having it matched.

Love brings more love. Don't ask yourself how you are going to get more love. Just be love, and allow the universe to guide you and give to you. The universe is always giving us what we feel we deserve. Now it's time to shape our future for our higher good.

Focusing on the Law of Attraction will help you become accountable to yourself. Now you're going to focus on how you sound to the universe. If it does not sound good and positive, it's not going to give you the outcome you want.

Stop the second guessing that gives off a negative vibe for the universe to work from. Come from a stronger, more powerful self and dream high.

When you want to empower your life, start with empowering others. Start to send good thoughts and energy to others. See how it can manifest within you. The more you can give the more you can receive. This will help you create the attraction you want.

When you send loving kindness it helps everyone involved. Start by smiling more at others, compliment people (and mean it!), or be of service when the opportunity is available. This positive action will raise your own energy and show others what good looks like.

When you encourage others, that positive energy will enhance your vibration. What you put out, you receive. The moment you become jealous your energy changes into a low vibration—and you may actually not affect them as much as you do yourself.

I know someone that would always think negative whenever she saw a slim, healthy person. She had a body and weight issue and would immediately become jealous. For her to help herself and support people with loving kindness, it was important for her to see a healthy person and honor them and see that they have success in the area that she would like improvement in.

Once she started to react with supportive energy, she no longer pushed away the energy she wanted to create in her own world. It's almost impossible to dislike energy in someone and want that same energy to open within yourself.

Create good karma by helping others. Look for opportunities that you can use to help better the people that you meet each day. This will help you be more aware of what's going on around you and notice when you can help others. The higher your vibration can get, the higher the gifts will be.

Keep yourself positive and in good standing with the universal gifts. Start hearing your words and be accountable for how you talk to yourself. Inside your mind and with your voice—everything is heard.

When your inside voice has a negative thought, it creates a negative outcome. That's the law. If you continue to say, "I don't want to be late," it tells the universe that you're only focused on being late. You have not required plan B. The universe does not have any judgment about your thought, so helping you create the lateness that you say you do not want is what the universe does.

A better thought would be, *I always arrive at the perfect time for me*. The universe hears that and will assist you in creating that perfect timing. Isn't it better to begin focusing on what you want, and have positive energy running around you?

If you think, *There is never enough money at the end of the month*, and that's your belief system, you will be 100% correct. The universe needs to create bigger bills and more moments that will use up any extra money you might manage to save. It will give you what you state as your truth.

If you changed your story to, *I have and always will have enough money each and every month*, your results will be amazing. Good things will start to come your way. You will have the universe aligned with your real desires and not your fear-based worries. This is when the Law of Attraction is working with you and not against you.

There was this client that I had not seen for a couple years. I was invited to her home and I witnessed that she was doing very well for herself and her family.

WOW, she's doing fantastic and she has just shown me that I too can dream higher. If I want to achieve more like she has, I just have to write this into my story. Moments like these can shift your vibration into a good experience or a jealous and negative experience. I now choose to have a positive and blessed experience. I see my client's success story as achievable within my life and I honor her energy and thank her for showing me more.

When I left her presence, I was motivated to get outside my comfort zone and hit another level. I believe the universe put me into her home to show me another level that I could achieve, and I was ready.

See other people's success stories as a way of lighting up your success ladder. They are not showing off, they are just being who they have designed themselves to be. They can either light up or dim your ladder to success. It will always be your call and your choice.

When a client comes in wanting to attract a life partner, it's important that they just tell me what they want. I, along with the universe, do not want or need to hear what you *do not want* to manifest. Remember, that lights up the negative energy and if it's entertained at all, it's going to be manifested!

Tell me what you want. Keep your stories clean. Be positive and that is all the information the universe will hear and work from. Your story does not need to start out with: *I don't want a cheater, I don't want a smoker, I don't want a bad job, I don't want a bum and I'm tired of bad relationships.* It may have been your truth recently, but if you don't change the story, you will keep getting the same kind of relationships and jobs.

A clean story might sound like this: *I want a healthy, loving man, that has a good solid life and that wants a beautiful relationship, I want a job that I enjoy going to.* That sounds like a wonderful order to send out to the universe and it will get you the result you desire.

Now think about a few things that you have wanted to manifest and how you can reword your thoughts to match your truth. Do this exercise when you feel good about you and you are excited to shift into more greatness. This is helpful in all areas of your life. We are in control of being successful in all areas of our lives.

I had an old story that I owned for a long time. I would tell people that I'm hardcore when it comes to the gym. When I was going, I would attend up to ten times a week. I loved working out at the gym. But my story did not produce the outcome I wanted. If I missed a couple days, then you would not see me for years. I would completely stop. A couple of years later I would continue this story and start again, then stop again. Of course something had to happen to keep my story real. I would have to create a moment that would make me stop.

One day I started to listen to someone talk about the gym and I got motivated again. My story repeated itself and I decided right then and there I wanted to create a different story around my workouts. I needed a story that worked for me long-term and that would help me achieve my real goal.

This time I told myself that the old story I had been keeping alive did not serve my higher needs or desires any longer. It was a negative story that I had outgrown. So I needed to create a new story that sounded like it would support me in what I really wanted, and that was to work out.

So my new story is: I just work out. Those four words for me have been the most powerful words that I have been able to attach to my workout story. It's so easy, so quick and yet so powerful. "I just work out" has given me a healthy story that supports my higher good. I have at times missed a couple of days and did not need to worry. I went back as soon as my life and my schedule would allow. I changed one story and that was life altering.

I just work out is a long term success story that works for me.

* * *

Sometimes our intent is in the right place, but we don't use the right words to attract what we really want. Let's look at a few examples of flipping the coin to make sure you are attracting and asking for the right things from the universe.
Instead of saying or thinking:

- I don't want to date a person who is unfaithful.
- I would like a new job, but I don't want to work long hours.
- I don't want to be late for work.
- I want to lose weight.
- I want to be debt free.
- I want to be less stressed and less worried all the time.
- Don't forget to…

Try flipping the coin and say/think:

- I date a loyal person.
- I would like a new job that offers the perfect hours for my schedule.
- I will arrive to work at the right time.
- I want to be fit and healthy.
- I want to have a surplus of money.
- I want to feel happy and content now and about the future.
- Remember to…

Try to understand how we really need to focus on just a few key words that the universe will understand and you will then attract. The sentence, "I want to lose weight," seems like a great thought and desire. However, when we break down this thought into key words we end up with *lose* and *weight*. Individually, these words have a negative connotation. The universe will hear that because it doesn't see the whole sentence, just the key words. So, instead think *I want to be fit and healthy.* Now the universe hears the words *fit* and *healthy*, and now you will attract this.

What thoughts no longer serve your higher self?

What story do you want to own from now on?

Manifesting personal goals
I no longer need to want, I just create.

We can't achieve our goals without first creating them. Setting goals will keep you in the process of continually forging a new and more positive outcome in your life. It's all about staying in the game and being a winner.

Without a goal we have no reference point for determining how we are doing; no way of knowing where we are and where we want to go in life. Once you embrace the power of goal making, you will start to see a shift in your life that will springboard you into high levels of achievement.

The practice of setting and meeting goals can be a very powerful tool for making positive changes in your life. Begin by first believing in yourself— that you can change your life's outcome. Create goals that represent things in your life that you have been wanting. Now is the time to start manifesting these things. This will get your energy to start aligning with your new wants.

Goals will help you live up to your full potential and become accountable for your life. It's important to look at the areas of your life that you are not content with and change them. It's time to no longer just wish for the changes. It's time to let go of your self-doubts and create the life that you have wanted to live.

It's easier at times to stay in your old stuck ways. I understand it takes some energy and time to write a new story. I also know that every time you step out of your old story that does not work anymore, it's worth it.

Now is the time to stop complaining about what you don't have and start creating what you want. I personally get drained listening to people talk about how hard life is and how bad it is to not be happy. It's time to write that one goal that will propel you into creating and reaching more and more goals.

Typically, a goal is written down and then actions are needed to start creating the outcome you desire. This can be amazingly easy once you get the mindset and put positive energy behind it. Enjoy making your goals. See yourself enjoying the progress from point A to point B. This alone will start to get your energy vibration behind your goals. Without enjoying the process it's hard to want to stay on track.

Now let's learn how to energetically charge your goals for a more successful outcome. The universe is behind you, wanting to create a positive world for you and others. This will be the power source that can amplify the success of your outcome.

A lot of people want to create more prosperity and abundance but don't know how to write a new story that is not based on their previous limiting beliefs. The key point to remember when you are manifesting your new goals is to see yourself in present-time information, and not in your past stories or fear-based future stories. You only exist in the present-time. Your past hurts cannot influence your story. Your future fears do not need to reduce your goals. When you are in the moment and feeling positive in nature and strong in spirit, you are ready to create a new reality.

The universe is here to help you write a better success story that will give you the outcome you desire. Meditate on your real desires and then define the goals that you want to achieve. Meditate on seeing your goals from start to finish and enjoy the process.

When you start a goal make sure that you can visualize the finished outcome. If you can't see the finished outcome then it's hard to see the worthiness of the work. Dream high and get excited! This will give you the accountability that is needed to see completion.

Keep your eye on the prize. When a goal is important to you, then you will want to enjoy the whole process. A goal should be enjoyable, especially the finished outcome. Staying focused on the prize means that you will keep this charged with positive energy. When you lose that focus, the desire tends to seep away.

See your goals as being on a target. When I focus on a target all other thoughts and distractions go away. I get deeply into what I want my outcome to be. I can now give my goals all the energy and attention they need in order to keep them alive within me. I get locked in on what I want and I stay focused on the outcome I desire. When this happens, I do not allow distractions to come into my awareness, getting me off track. In this moment I become stronger in my own power. Being powerful in your life and in your actions can make you the winner you now accept.

See your goal as 100% achievable. This creates the vibration of success. Look around at the successful people you meet and match their energy. They run success energy in that area. An athletic person runs healthy energy. They don't roll out of bed and ask themselves if they will be healthy and successful again. They just run that energy. They have created a goal and now live it daily with little or no effort. It becomes their story and their automatic response to life. They already know the vibration that is needed to match the outcome they set out to accomplish. That is why winners like to be around other winners. The vibrations that they run are comfortable to each other.

Be confident in your goal setting. Meditate on the steps needed, see the end results, and enjoy the process. Then allow the universe to align you. Realize that you don't need to know all the answers to every step. The universe will fill in the gaps. It's understandable that you do not know how to accomplish the goal you have not achieved yet.

The universe wants you to be successful. Write the story in such a way that you know what you want as the end result. Believe that it's that easy. Be open to the universe guiding you in the direction that is needed. It's important for you to write your story and for the universe to assist you. Becoming aligned with the higher energy will make your goals even grander than you thought possible.

At times we do not know how to dream high. We dream with limitations that have been pre-programmed in us. Perhaps you have been told, "Don't get all excited," or, "Don't expect too much or you will get hurt." These have fear-based energy attached to them.

Learn to dream. And then allow the universe to take the dreams to another level of greatness. Be open to receiving information on all levels. Your thoughts may be heightened; especially your third eye will become open to seeing new things. Work with your third ear and hear your own inner voice directing you. You may also have people give you some amazing leads or new people come into your life and bring you new insight. Open your mind, and shift into a new you. Become a magnet for the energy to flow through you and into your physical world. Magic can happen at these levels.

In order to be successful, we need to be open for change. You cannot allow the same old actions that have been keeping you away from these new and exciting thoughts. It's the perfect time to redesign yourself. Be open to new ideas and to new people coming into your life with exactly the information you're looking for. This will intensify your outcome.

If a client were to come to me to stop drinking, I could take away his cravings within minutes through energy work. But if I don't work on his habits and automatic responses, then he will want to do the same thing he has been doing forever, even though he truly no longer wants to do so. Whether he has cravings for a drink or not, his habitual act of going and getting a drink is worse than the drinking itself. I also need to change the habits of the man. He needs to redesign his automatic responses of going to get a drink. Creating a new healthier automatic response will help him rewrite his story, stay in power and be successful.

Examine yourself. See what areas of your life will no longer fit into your new higher self. Fix your automatic responses by coming up with healthier ways of living your life. Become proactive. This will instantly start to line yourself up with a new higher you. A successful you!

All these steps will greatly improve your life and make your goals become your new reality, launching you into your final step of success.

Accept the gifts you have created. You know you have the power to create your dreams, now remember to accept these gifts. The universe is and has always has been on your side. Shift into accepting, receiving and embracing the gifts of your work.

Your gifts can be from anyone, any place and at any time. When you get a special price on an item, win a gift or have special treatment from someone, see it as a gift. Thank the universe for always watching and providing. The universe has gifted me many ways that I had not expected.

Help shows up in all forms: a gift from a friend, a huge sale on an item you want, a phone call that made you smile, or a text when you needed that person's strength. Be open and be thankful in all moments of time.

What are you ready to manifest?

What areas do you want to start changing right now?

Hypnotherapy

My mind now speaks my truth.

Hypnotherapy helps the mind and body connect together on a deeper level and release pictures that no longer serve a need. When the mind says one thing and the body wants another, it creates a disconnect. Hypnotherapy brings balance and corrects what is not working. This is a beautiful way of canceling out the inside voice that limits you from moving forward and frees you from those things that do not serve your higher self. When you learn to let go of old patterns that no longer serve your higher self, change can be simple.

Some people have fear-based energy about being hypnotized and losing control. When you can trust the experience and the moment, you relax into a new awareness.

The client is always in control and knows what is going on at all times.

A professional hypnotherapist does not want you to lose control, but to merge into a different kind of control that will balance you. During a normal session the body is completely aware of the surroundings. You will know who you are, that you are in full control, and will be able to act and keep yourself safe.

Some people can go very deep into relaxation during a session—*still fully aware and able to react*—some go very light, and most stay in the middle. When you are relaxed and in a dreamlike state the mind is more accepting of new ideas. That's when you can most easily hear the new information and embrace it as your truth. It's almost like a mind reset. Before each session I find out what words and thoughts work for you as an individual person. Then feed you those thoughts that will shift you upward.

Being able to correct the inner dialog that wants to control the outer dialog is crucial. The more we learn and empower our automatic thoughts, the more we learn how powerful our inner voice really is. Getting rid of the negative voices, turning them into positive, will empower you to shift into a life that is working *for* you and not *against* you.

* * *

A young lady came in to my office wanting and needing chocolate two to three times a day. Her body and mind knew it was not a healthy choice, but her inside voice was very powerful. The more she seemed to try to drown out that negative voice, the stronger the desire became.

She came in for one session, asking to get rid of her chocolate addiction/cravings. I mentioned to her that chocolate could be healthy in the right amount. I then asked her what a healthy amount of chocolate might be for her. Her answer was two to three times per week.

I was able to hypnotize her easily so that she could change her inner voice that was controlling her. We set up the new belief that she now wanted to and would enjoy eating chocolate two to three times per week and feel okay with this action. After the session she only wanted and craved chocolate a couple of times per week, but could mostly go without it.

Once the body and mind were on the same page they could cohabitate together without problems. Her shift was easy, quick and beautiful. The body and mind want to and can work together to create a healthier outcome.

Hypnosis can help people in all areas of their lives, from addiction to phobias. We know all issues reside in the subconscious and can be shifted. Our goal is to have our thoughts suit our needs. Rethinking our patterns and questioning our truths helps us bring our best into action.

* * *

A smoker that does not want to stop will not have a successful session. You have to personally want the change, for the change to happen. No one can walk into my office wanting to change for another person. They need to be invested enough to make real changes happen on a personal level.

Hypnosis changes your inner voice to match healthier desires. You may have had moments in your past that did not play out the way you wanted and that created a new disconnect. In hypnosis we can go in and change the energy of that event. Pain is released and you can move forward with no pain attached, allowing you to move on.

For example, say you didn't pass a driver's test and then became unable to move through that feeling of failure. A hypnotherapy session can clear that blockage. If you reach out for help soon after a moment like that, the shift is easier and faster. If you sit in your fear for months or years, that fear becomes deeply rooted and can spread into other areas, requiring a deeper session.

People tend to have past stories that continue to play in their minds and that lower their self-esteem. Removing and healing these stories can release you from past blocks, opening up a greater sense of self.

If you have always felt like you were not the smart one in the family or at school, that information can play out in your adult world. This can create a huge negative belief system that festers, keeping you trapped and unable to move forward. It may or may not have been your truth, but if it continues, it becomes your downfall.

Hypnosis can release your emotions, allowing you to move past a negative story and create a healthier future. Correcting that little voice, bringing it into a healthier understanding of truth, can create the power one needs to heal and move forward.

It's important to correct and release your past information. This opens you up to redesigning the new you from a powerful place. Again, you are not your past story, you are present-time without a history. With hypnosis, you can erase negative information and write a powerful updated story.

* * *

When you listen to your mind you will live it out. I had a client come in that had not slept well in three days. She repeatedly told me she knew she could not sleep. She knew her body needed sleep but her mind was convinced she could not sleep. I laughed inside knowing that her own words were completely opposite of her desires. She was not allowing herself to sleep. All I had to do was to get her to relax enough to change the story that bound her to the dysfunction. I asked for her smartphone and recorded a quick hypnosis for her to listen to when she went to bed.

As I did the recording I looked at her and was able to hold her gaze. With a voice of authority I spoke to her in a way that commanded her to stay focused on each word I was going to say. I told her she would go to bed in and around her bedtime and fall asleep. She would occasionally awake, roll over and then go right back to sleep. Around the time she needed to get up, she would wake up feeling rested.

I did not need to take her into a deep hypnotic state since she had only been dealing with this issue for 3 days. I was able to create enough presence for her to believe in my words and to correct her story in an awakened state. Hypnosis can be achieved in a non-hypnotic state of awareness.

Hypnosis is nothing to be feared. Our minds have so much control over how we create our lives. As a hypnotherapist, I listen to the words used and shift the story to something that is worthy of being lived out.

A traditional session starts by helping you break down the occasion when a negative moment became powerful enough to create a negative outcome that stuck with you. Then we see what other areas this might have damaged or contaminated. We rewrite that area of pain into a positive by diffusing that part of you that has stayed wounded.

Once the story has been shifted, you are ready to become deeply relaxed and able to hear your new and empowered information. The shift can be very quick and easy, or at other times it might take a few days to percolate into your life. A recording of the session for you to listen to later will help focus on your new belief about yourself.

* * *

I worked on a client who did not believe that she could be really successful. She even sabotaged herself many times in jobs and in business. Bringing out her old family hurt and pain helped her see herself at her current body's age with no old limitations. The shift in her self-esteem helped her grow into who she really desired to be. Her happiness level increased and her life became more worth living.

The more we become okay with our past, the more we can become stronger in our lives. Our organic selves are powerful. This is who we are. Anything less is a past issue clouding up present-time.

* * *

People tend to label themselves. I'm too fat, I'm lazy, I can't do anything right. The inner dialog is powerful and it reflects itself into our present-time lives. If your mind is convinced that the words you use have truth, then it is your truth. These stories need to be looked at, corrected and rewritten into stories that are based on present-time information.

Going into the subconscious mind while being relaxed and open to receiving is a powerful life changing moment. This is why hypnosis is a fast way of releasing you from your negative you.

Winners win because they know winning as truth. You can have a powerful life when your inner voice truly is in balance with your potential!

What area would I like to improve in?

What actions can you do right now that will help you in your future?

Case studies

Finding help can be one of your greatest moves.

I work on so many people that come in with a negative story that they just can't seem to let go of. Once they have been told they have a certain issue, disease or condition, they hold on to it forever. It may be their present-time truth, but it does not need to be their future truth. I tell them to look at this information as a guide to the things they want to work on, not as a life sentence.

Here's a personal example. A while ago I tore the muscles and ligaments in my left wrist so badly that I thought it was broken. I went to my doctor and he said it was quite serious. This accident happened on a Monday night. The doctor's information I received was on Tuesday morning.

I did not want to hear the doctor's time frame for my recovery, because I knew I could heal much faster.

That Tuesday I went into agreement to heal my wrist on or before Saturday morning. I woke up Saturday and had full use of my wrist. I know I can heal myself with energy, but I also need the belief system that it can happen.

The stories below are from a few of my clients that came to me wanting change. They may not have known exactly what they needed, but they knew they needed to change. I was able to hear their stories and change the energy connected to the unwanted outcomes. Change is easy once you open yourself to receiving a better outcome.

Cher, a 53 year old woman, came in because she could not walk without her cane.

She was unable to do anything and could hardly take a shower because she was in so much physical pain. Her appointment was for a massage but once I looked at her, I knew most of her physical body pain was actually emotional pain.

I asked her to sit down so I could work on her emotional body, and then we would work on her physical body through a massage. I cleaned out her aura which was extremely depleted of energy. You can't heal or move forward when you are depleted. I cleaned out her chakras so that she could start to own her personal power. She had given away her sense of power to others and had nothing to give to herself.

Once I read her energy and told her why she was getting the results she was getting, she felt less confused about her personal life. She actually made more sense to herself. Her mind was now able to see a better outcome. Before this she had a belief that she would not get better.

I started the massage face down so I could check out the sciatica that she said was her issue. I realized that her whole back was completely frozen with fear-based energy that locked up her muscles. I actually had to tell her to just be quiet and to stop being wimpy.

I had to use a strong voice that commanded authority for her to settle down. Once she heard me take charge, she settled down. This told me that she had more control over her body then she realized. A few minutes later I asked her to roll over onto her back. She rolled over but stayed propped up on her elbows, saying she couldn't lay flat because of her vertigo and back pain. Again I was firm, giving her a direct order, telling her that she could and would lie down and she'd be fine.

Cher went into full agreement with me and did as I requested. Again, this let me know that she had more control over her body than she believed. We did a couple of minutes of stretching and I was done. The healing she needed was not a physical body healing, but an emotional body healing.

Before I left the room I asked her to get up from the massage table; telling her in my command voice, "You will get up off the table and be in little or no pain. You will be able to get dressed and walk out of my massage room into the front area without your cane. You will also be able to walk around in the front area with little or no pain. Do you understand what I just said to you?" She said she did. Then I said, "I will take your cane with me, is that okay?" She didn't have a problem with my doing so.

Cher walked out of my massage room with little or no pain. She was able to walk around the front area and sit down with little or no pain. I gave her back her cane and told her for safety she may want to use it for the stairs but she would not need it again for the rest of the day. She was amazed that she could do everything I said she could do and she went home, significantly more productive and focused in her life.

In this story I want to you understand that when our minds hold on to limitations, our body will respond to and match that vibration. When you tell your body you can't do something, you own it. If you are not careful, you get stuck in that low vibration and it becomes your future.

Know that your body wants to heal, and it's time now to start working your whole mind, body, and spirit connection for a full recovery. Please monitor your inside words, work on your aura and chakras to match what's in your outside world.

* * *

Jack heard about me and wanted to see if I could help him with the Bell's Palsy that he had suffered from for nearly two years.

He was 52 years old. His condition was so bad that he had to tape his right eye closed at night to keep it from drying out. The entire right side of his face was paralyzed and the muscles sagged, giving him a one-sided smile that he was very self-conscious about. His speech was slurred and his eye wept and watered constantly. There was a part of him that believed he was never going to get better, even though it was his goal to get better. His inner voice was fear-based and his doctors said they could do nothing to help him.

I started working on his energy to bring it into a high healing vibration. I worked on all his chakras and his aura to bring them back into a healthier space. He was depleted of energy which was why his body could not handle this issue. Within 30 minutes of cleaning out his energy, his speech had become better. He noticed his words were clearer and it was easier to pronounce them. His eye stopped weeping and he felt tingling in the right side of his face. He called me two days later and said the healing was continuing, that his eyes were now working together and he could even blink both eyes at the same time!

Jack was worried that his body could not heal itself, so his body went into agreement to keep creating what he feared he would have forever. I was able to increase his energy so that his body could balance out and heal. The healing was almost instant. The energy body went into agreement to become healthy—that's the easy part. Getting the mind to accept the healing might take longer. I had to override his doctor's information that his body would not heal. Once I worked on his emotional body, it took the physical body just a couple of days to shift into alignment with the healthy energy body.

Within a few days the right side of his mouth was able to contribute to his smile. It took a little while for his body to rebuild the muscles so that the smile was completely even, but the process of healing was finally there.

* * *

Ed, who's 51 years old, also had Bell's Palsy. He only had symptoms for a couple of weeks and already had huge signs of improvement. He just felt that he needed some assistance to speed up the process.

When he came in to see me he was hungry to change his condition. That's half of the healing. He said he was not going to put up with his Bell's Palsy. He had already written his success story and just needed more energy to speed up the healing process.

I was able to give his body the excess energy he needed to go in and rebalance the body. After his session, his face was almost back to normal. I was able to work with him and his energy and help him create his positive outcome.

His session was so different than most. He knew he was going to get better and just needed assistance. His body was very accepting of change and embraced the process. He also understood that this issue was tied to an emotion that needed to be looked at. Things like this tend to happen to awaken us to look at our lives and change. He embraced all aspects of change.

* * *

Seventeen-year old Bryan was brought in by his mom, a registered nurse. He suffered from a lot of emotional issues caused by trauma in his childhood and was on a lot of strong medications for PTSD (Post Traumatic Stress Disorder) and ADHD (Attention Deficit Hyperactivity Disorder). When he walked into my office he apologized for his behavior, stating that it was hard to meet strangers and difficult to go to a new place and feel safe.

He had to be home schooled because he didn't feel safe or comfortable at school. He also said he could not look at me. He just looked around my office and avoided any eye contact. I could sense he was scared and frightened just being in a new environment. We stood at the door for 20 minutes because I wanted to make him feel safe before he actually walked in to sit down.

I didn't have to talk to him about his past, those stories that continued to play in his head and kept him frozen in his story. It was time to override his negative thoughts and give him positive thoughts to move forward with.

I worked with his aura to bring it in closer so he could feel safer. (People with boundary issues tend to have a wide aura.) I cleaned out the information in his chakras so he wouldn't run the same old stories that were not serving his higher self.

I noticed within an hour that he was able to have full eye contact with me, to laugh, to smile, and that his nervousness was gone. I witnessed him being a normal teenage kid. He was coming from present-time and in his present-time, he was safe. It was a beautiful moment, seeing him shift so much in so little time.

His PTSD kept his negative past emotions open. It was important to make him feel safe and good in the moment. By cleaning out his aura and chakras to release the negative energy, I brought him into a safe place. When he could be in the moment, he could just be himself and not the wounded person he had held on to. He was not bound to reliving his traumas with every breath, he was just being what the moment allowed him to be and that was just a 17-year old. He was even able to give me a hug when he left. I asked him to step out so I could talk to his mom before he left. As he walked out, she started to cry. She had never seen her son change so quickly and look so carefree.

* * *

My youngest daughter, Erin, was three years old and hospitalized in a small rural hospital in northern California. She started out with flu-like symptoms, and within a couple days became so dehydrated that she needed to be taken to an emergency hospital. There it was determined that she had a severe blood infection. Her white blood cell count was over 30,000 and she had to be airlifted to the closest pediatrics hospital.

I was a Reiki Grandmaster at the time and was able to do hands on healing to help give her body the extra energy it needed to balance itself out. I crawled into the crib and kept my hands on her for five straight days. Within one month, her blood tested beautifully.

Reiki raises the hemoglobin of the blood, creating more oxygen to run throughout the body. Her body was able to heal much faster with the Reiki treatments. I am very thankful I learned Reiki. A man at Stanford Hospital had a similar case a week before my daughter came down with the virus. He did not survive it.

* * *

I was at an OfficeMax waiting for a manager when a young clerk 30 feet away told me she had a headache. I laughed and ask if she would like to get rid of her headache. She looked at me kind of confused and said she wanted to get rid of her headache. I stayed where I was and focused on her energy. I noticed her energy was congested. Within three minutes, not telling her who I was or what I do, I was able to release her headache. The minute I was done, she turned and looked at me and said her headache was gone.

This was a quick and easy healing. She did not know who I was so she did not worry what I was going to do, she did not judge the outcome or hold on to her headache information. I noticed her energy was congested so I just released all excess energy in and around the head. Within a couple of minutes, staying 30 feet away from her, I was able to quickly release the energy that was creating her pain.

* * *

Andy had been coming to me for massages for about two years. He was 43 years old, stressed with family and work issues and had problems with his back. He also had a tumor that kept growing back after two surgeries to remove it. It was growing in and around his spine and the doctors told him he would need further surgeries to keep it from becoming too big of a mass. They also told him that he would probably be paralyzed at some point, since the growth was growing around the spine.

I knew about his tumor and had worked on the scars that were created by the surgeries. I did not do a lot of additional work on the tumor area but he was able to receive huge results.

After two years of coming to me monthly he had another tumor checkup was very excited to hear that he was tumor free! After going through surgeries and checkups for over six years, and being told he could end up being paralyzed, he was finally free of worry. His body no longer had any signs of a tumor on his spine. His next appointment, he told me he thought it was because of my healing hands and body work.

I did not see his tumor as an issue. I worked on breaking up the scar tissue that was tightening up his lower back and relaxing his whole physical and emotional body. I know when you can let go of stress the body has more energy to go in and heal itself.

* * *

Lisa was a 15 year old girl who suffered from bulimia and self-cutting. Her bulimia was so bad she had to go to the doctor weekly to be weighed. Her mom brought her in. Lisa was full of attitude and completely disengaged, sitting with her arms crossed, looking at the ceiling. I asked her mom to step outside so I could work on her without any distractions.

She had a lot of control issues with her mom as well as there being additional family dynamics involved. Once I listened to her needs and validated her, she started to relax. I cleaned out her negative stuck energy, and we were able to look at how she could fit into the family from her own perspective. Once she settled down and softened, she could find balance within herself.

Within 30 minutes she was laughing and completely engaged in our conversation. Her mom came back and I was able to bridge the gap between them. While reading her energy I was able to tell her a lot about herself so that she was able to understand why she was feeling so left out. During her session, I did not bring up the bulimia or the cutting. That's generally the outcome of the situation and not the cause.

Just before she left, I looked at her and thought to myself, *Oh wait, what about the eating issue?* I looked at her energy and said with confidence, "Just eat." She laughed and responded, "Okay." She went home and gained four pounds that week and stopped cutting herself.

People with bulimia or cutting behavior have little or no say in their personal lives. Once I was able to clean her energy out and make her feel good about herself, she did not need to continue her negative behavior. It's important to value who you are, not how you feel others see you. Once she felt good about herself, she balanced out. It's critical that you do not allow family or friends to make you feel devalued.

* * *

Lane was a 38 year old scientist who did not believe in energy work. One day he hurt his thumb so badly that after two hours he went to go to the emergency room to have a hole drilled in the nail to relieve the pressure. I offered him some Reiki energy and his response was, "Okay, whatever."

I had him sit down on the floor in front of me and hold his hand up so that I could surround his thumb with my hands. I cupped the area but had no physical contact. At seven minutes a huge relief came over him. His whole body relaxed from the pain. His body was able to accept the healing energy and go in and release the pain and pressure. He said 80% of the pain was gone and he had just light throbbing that was manageable. His mind could not understand what had happened but his body was able to receive the energy and go into agreement to heal at a much faster rate than normal.

Even though he did not believe in my energy work, his healing was amazing. It was not a belief system I had to create in him. All he needed to do was just experience the process.

* * *

Adam was a heavy construction worker. His sister called and asked me to do a long distance Reiki treatment on him. His physical body did not need to be in my prescence. I was able to call in his energy body for a remote healing. She didn't tell him that she had called me for a session.

I asked her for his first and last name, his age and what area he lived in. That afternoon I sat down and called his energy body in to begin work on him. I had no information on why he needed treatments.

When I started to work on his stomach area, using a pillow as a proxy, I could sense his body starting to move even though he was not physically present in the room. The whole stomach area started to gurgle and move. I worked on his stomach area longer than I normally would because I felt that he needed it. Once the stomach area settled down I was able to move on.

I received a call from his sister the next day and she said that he was doing very well after his treatment. She filled me in on the fact that he had recently been run over by a bulldozer and his organs had been pushed over to one side making him look pregnant. He had been having multiple surgeries to repair his body and was spending days in the hospital after each procedure before feeling strong enough to go home.

This time, after the Reiki treatment on the day of his procedure, the doctors were able to save his colon and he was strong enough to go home.

His body was traumatized and depleted of energy. During the Reiki he was able to receive the extra energy needed to go in and build up his body for the surgery. His body was able to handle the surgery and heal much faster. The body wants to heal; all it needs is time and energy. Reiki gave him the energy he needed to go in, repair itself and heal his body.

* * *

Lupe was a 56 year old wife and mom who came in with Chronic Fatigue Syndrome, a condition that left her unable to do everyday things. She wasn't able to go to the grocery store. She didn't have enough energy to even bake a cake. If she did, she would have to lie down for the rest of the day.

Her daughter brought her in to see me. I did a Reiki session on her and she felt great afterwards. Once I got her to feel better, she became more open to the idea of becoming healthy. She wanted to learn to work on herself so I taught her first and second degree Reiki. Within weeks she was back to her normal healthy self. Within a month she had my daughters and I over for a tea party. Her daughter thanked me for helping her mom heal and balance. She now has a mom that can do things again.

Once a doctor tells a person that they have a disease they go into agreement with that story. It's important to understand that it does not have to remain part of your long-term story. It may be your present-time information but it does not have to be a life story or a life time sentence. The body can change and heal itself.

* * *

Rhonda, a 47 year old divorced mom with two adult children, came in with a fear of drowning, too much time spent daydreaming, and an inability to finish tasks. She just seemed to flounder her way through life dealing with petty distractions.

I did a Spiritual Transpersonal Release Technique Healing to dissolve all the past life influences that were clouding her present-time life. This form of therapy helped her focus and become more grounded.

She left feeling a sense of empowerment. She no longer had any fear of drowning and she understood why she was always distracted from her tasks. She now has a strong drive to create a powerful future.

It's important to be able to clean up all past life karma and past life influences that do not serve your higher purpose in this lifetime. I was able to take the information that clouded her thoughts and that she no longer needed to live through. Once she was fully in this lifetime, her productivity increased and she no longer lived through a cloud of distractions.

Begin creating a belief system where you have more control over the outcome of your stories. We know now that we create a lot of our reality. It's time to invest in yourself and your life.

You are the only one responsible and in charge of your happiness. So, if you are not fulfilled in life, look in the mirror and see where you are and where you want to be. Bridge that gap.

Dream high and believe in yourself. Do the work needed to change your story and its outcome. It really is that easy and that effortless.

What questions does this chapter bring up for me?

What actions can I take that serve my higher self?

Bring it all together

There's a time and space when you're just ready for change.

Creating change is a mindset; one that can help you want a better you. This is the time when you're just going to do it. No more waiting for the right moment or finding another excuse. Time is too precious to waste.

Your purchase of this book and investing your time in reading it tells me you're ready. Now let's get action behind your words so you can help yourself manifest a new world.

Life is all about change, empowerment and becoming more of your authentic self.

When you wake up every morning, your old habits will tend to create the same old outcome that you now desire to change.

But now, you can begin each morning by changing your old patterns. Start every morning wanting to challenge your automatic actions. Keep your goals close, your body healthy and your actions positive.

A successful person rarely wastes a beautiful day. Your daily actions can make your life better or make it stagnate. From now on, focus on making your actions support the new higher vibrational person you require yourself to be.

This is the time to question your drive and motivation. You know you can achieve greatness. You also know what it takes to manifest a new change. Meditation, cleaning and working with your chakras, believing in yourself, and changing your inner dialog will support your new ways. So, believe in yourself and choose the actions that will benefit you right now. Wake up earlier each day and begin to invest in yourself. The payoff will be beautiful.

We tend to wake up during the work week and invest in our jobs and then we often waste our days off being unproductive. When your time is yours, be productive for yourself. Your days off are when you want to inspire yourself to invest in your dreams. This alone will give you a new focus on what is really important. Your days off are now your time to be invested in your own needs.

A large majority of our lives will be spent in the working world. So, the time spent in the workforce needs to be the best that we can create. Knowing our energy is being affected in each moment means that our work environment has a powerful effect on our overall wellbeing.

We know we manifest in all areas of our lives and work is part of our manifestation. Have you done the best you can when it comes to your job or career? Do you need to become more accepting of the current situation, or do you need to change this part of your life?

What will most help your overall sense of self? Look deep inside and find the courage to be fully blessed. You may or may not need to change a job or career, but your energy about work might need to change. Always do your best. You may need a small, or a major, shift in this area.

The question that needs to be asked is: *What can I do to start changing and moving forward?* Once a step is made the vibration rises. Meditate on step one and don't focus on how to do step eight or twelve. Step one is your starting point and the universe will give you the information and assistance you need for the other steps. When you really think about it, one step is easy. It's one step at a time. As for the other steps, you will be energetically guided.

Moving forward in any area of your life starts a shift in the right direction. In the previous chapter, you've been given some examples on how others have improved themselves. It's time to create your own change. Think how delicious it would be to fully enjoy your job or have a career that you are emotionally, mentally, and physically in agreement with. This is within reach.

Close your eyes and see yourself running healthy energy throughout your day. What kind of energy are you used to running? Now that you know the importance and the magnitude of your ways, you will want to be the change.

* * *

Let's look at relationships. This can be a huge part of your emotional health. When we struggle in a relationship, our whole sense of self can become compromised. We may allow our boundaries to be pushed on and we then become smaller in life. When we become smaller, it's easier to stay in a bad situation. This will no longer be easy for you to do. What you know will now require you to want more. Using the tools I have provided can create a stronger person in you.

If you are single, then just love yourself. Allow yourself to be comfortable being single. Relax and build a strong you that can be happy in all moments of your life. Stop creating the need for something that is not present in your world.

Once you master self-love you can attract love into your life. Focus on self-love and embody loving-kindness. This will spread throughout all areas of your life. Love will soften your energy and help you attract more loving energy into your life.

If you are in a low vibrational relationship with a partner, it's important to find out what actions are needed to grow back into self-love. You can't grow with love and be in an unhappy relationship. We always have options and now we can make the changes necessary for happiness. We choose happiness that will benefit all areas of our lives.

Becoming real with yourself will help you come up with the actions that are needed. Relationships can hit so many levels of emotions. Where are you within the boundaries of being healthy? Be the example of self-love and require yourself to want better.

The more you understand how all of these areas affect you, the hungrier you will be for change. Ask yourself, and meditate on, what changes will be best for all involved. If you want to improve your love for your mate, then just love unconditionally. Feel how good it feels to relax and be less judgmental.

* * *

A client of mine made a choice to open up with her husband about her needs. In her opening up, he understood what she needed and he was there for her. The relationship between them changed almost overnight. All she needed to do was to be open, and all he needed to do was to understand her.

If you are in a relationship that does not serve your higher self or the people around you, then it's time to open up and see what changes are needed. It's time to no longer hide behind a life or relationship that is not working.

I understand working through issues is tough. Look at the process as being in the eye of the storm. It gives you some comfort from the storm but is keeping you trapped. Push through the storm and come out as a winner.

People all the time come to me and say they want to be happy but they don't have the courage to change. You now know that you cannot find the happiness you desire by being in a relationship that does not serve you well. Life takes courage.

On the other side of this coin is your happiness. Flip the coin, create the story of your success and be open to the signs the universe will give you. You are not alone, the universe is on your side waiting for you to want more.

* * *

Money can be a huge issue for some. Money can make us feel like we are 100% in control of our lives or 100% out of control. Looking at this area and seeing whether you need a change will give you peace of mind. When your finances are balanced your energy can relax and your creativity can grow. Fear stops the energy flow.

So many people overspend or don't make enough money to create the life they think they deserve. This is a real disconnect. It's time to look at all areas of our lives and start bringing them into balance. Money is an important area. No one owes you. You can be the rock you need to be and have the success you desire.

How do you view your self-worth? Are you emotionally hurting yourself in one or more areas of your life? Are you the one in control, the one who can shift and change? This might be a crucial moment in your life. If you are not happy, then change. The outcome of your change is coming into a healthy balance.

You can no longer blame the economy, your boss or your situation for creating your downfall. It was simply you settling with something that was not enough. Your body, your mind and your spirit are stronger than you may ever know. Don't settle for a low vibrational life. Expand your story to include an abundance of greatness.

Some people can make money and then spend it faster than they can bring it in. Learn to not fill your emotional emptiness with outside items. Once you get off the emotional roller coaster filled with emptiness, happiness will shift your energy. Once the shift takes place you can manifest the real gifts and then prosperity will find you.

Prosperity will find you when you are balanced and ready to receive. Positive energy is waiting in the background. The Law of Attraction and cleaning up your negative belief that money is hard to get will help you greatly.

* * *

Some people live with addictions. Spending too much money, smoking, drinking and anything in excess is a low vibration. Look at your world in a full 360-degree view and see what you can just say goodbye to. This means you are now demanding of yourself to require better. A lot of these area shifts really can be done in a split second and with little or no energy; especially when you create the mindset and the belief system that you deserve.

Looking at all areas that need to be shifted, see that change will happen when you become a healthier spirit on all levels. No one can require you to change. They can ask, plead and even beg, but it's just an illusion if you think this will result in long-term change.

This moment starts with you wanting to feel free in your life. Embrace success and move towards your dreams. Knowing when or where fear-based energy was first created is not important. Our focus is not in our past but in our future. It's all about moving forward in creating positive stories that we want to focus our energy on.

I want you to have fun writing your new stories.

* * *

I firmly believe that we are now in a time and place where we want to grow spiritually and find our ultimate happiness. The health of the world needs more people like you to raise the vibration of life.

This book has been written to introduce healthy alternative ways for self-empowerment and to help you begin to take action. I understand that many people do not know where to start or where to go and what modality can best help them move forward.

In this book, I have attempted to introduce you to a few very powerful modalities that you can embrace here and now; such as meditation, working with your energy system, the advantages of working with a life coach and the power of hypnosis. I have also included some stories of how people have shifted their lives, with little or no effort.

This is the moment when you take your first step and do that one thing that will help you. Just a single step can create a powerful outcome!

Does it take a little effort? Absolutely! Can you, and do you, have what it takes to apply one or two new concepts to your life? Yes, you do. And you know this is the perfect time to get outside your old self and become a gifted soul. Do the work for yourself, your family and loved ones.

I'm completely confident that you can become more invested in the future that you want, and that you crave the power of a positive change.

Now, in this moment of time, is when you take a deep breath and step into a healthier way to exist. You are, and will always be, far more powerful than what you can ever comprehend.

Take a moment right now to write down one to five steps that will best serve your present-time needs and then take the action needed to implement them.

Breathe, relax, and become excited for change and be the change. Be the person you have been born to be, the one that can move forward and have a take charge attitude.

I know this is the perfect time for you to shift and that our world needs stronger more likeminded people healing themselves and helping others to heal.

My dream is to inspire you for change.

May you enjoy your journey and your new beautiful self.

Namaste

Create your new story!

About the author

Diane S. Gysin, a professional psychic, healer, teacher and author, is the founder of the *Healing Bodies Healing Souls Wellness Center* in Fremont California. She has been studying energy and healing for over 25 years and has received over 15 certifications in different healing modalities.

Her goals are to continue learning about energy, teach others what she learns, and travel to different places in order to experience other ways of living.

She spends her time teaching meditation and energy work through speaking engagements and private, group and phone sessions.

You can reach her through:

> *www.HealingBodiesHealingSouls.com*
> Facebook: Healing Bodies Healing Souls
> Google: Healing Bodies Healing Souls
> DianeG6870@aol.com or 510.468.1641

Made in the USA
San Bernardino, CA
18 July 2015